DATE DUE

CITY
HALL
GOES
ABROAD

For my mother and in memory of my father

CITY
HALL
GOES
ABROAD

The Foreign Policy of Local Politics

HEIDI H. HOBBS

SAGE Publications
International Educational and Professional Publisher
Thousand Oaks   London   New Delhi

For information address:

SAGE Publications, Inc.
2455 Teller Road
Thousand Oaks, California 91320

SAGE Publications Ltd.
6 Bonhill Street
London EC2A 4PU
United Kingdom

SAGE Publications India Pvt. Ltd.
M-32 Market
Greater Kailash I
New Delhi 110 048 India

Printed in the United States of America

Library of Congress Cataloging-in-Publication Data

Hobbs, Heidi H.
  City hall goes abroad : the foreign policy of local politics /
Heidi H. Hobbs.
    p. cm.
  Includes bibliographical references and index.
  ISBN 0-8039-5522-7. — ISBN 0-8039-5523-5 (pbk.)
    1. Municipal government–United States–International cooperation.
    2. United States–Foreign relations–1989- I. Title.
JS323.H63 1994
352'.0072–dc20   93-43664
                                                          CIP

94 95 96 97 98 10 9 8 7 6 5 4 3 2 1

Sage Production Editor: Yvonne Könneker

Contents

Acknowledgments

This book has been a long time in coming and could not have been completed without the encouragement and support of so many people over the last few years. While I alone am responsible for the content, I would like to take this opportunity to note their contributions.

First and foremost, my positive experience at the University of Southern California School of International Relations must be recognized. My professors there, especially Gerald J. Bender, Harlan Hahn, and James N. Rosenau, were instrumental in seeing me through to graduation. Michael Fry, director of the school for most of my time there, also offered me tremendous support during my graduate school experience. In addition, a special acknowledgment must be made to Carole Gustin, who served the school in several capacities during my tenure there. The importance of her words of encouragement cannot be measured and will not be forgotten.

My graduate school experience would not have been the same without my two closest schoolmates, Craig C. Etcheson and Dario V. Moreno. Our friendship withstood three doctoral dissertations and subsequent professional development. My special thanks go out to these irreplaceable friends.

More recently, I have been supported in my endeavors through my current position in the department of political science at Illinois State University. Nancy Lind, Jamal Nassar, and Sherry Stephens have been particularly helpful to me in seeing this project through. Other people around the university who have been of great help as well include Nora Jones in academic computing; Roy Treadway, director of Census and Data Users; and Ann Cohen, director of the research office of the College of Arts and Sciences. The research and technical aspects of this document could not have been completed without their assistance.

Likewise, I was fortunate enough to attend an ICPSR-sponsored workshop on census data at the University of Michigan this past summer that was critical to the completion and updating of the data analysis for this book. I am most grateful to all who made the workshop possible and to the Illinois State University Grant Incentive Fund, which paid for my attendance.

Sage Publications has been very good to me. I am most thankful to Blaise Simqu, who first encouraged me to publish with Sage, and Carrie Mullen for seeing it through. I would also like to thank two anonymous reviewers for Sage who offered particularly helpful comments.

Finally, all the work we do is a product of our personal happiness. I have been very fortunate over the years to have colleagues, friends, and family who have supported me throughout my graduate and professional career. Their close contact has enabled me to survive the academic jungle. While a simple listing of their names is not sufficient, let them stand in recognition for their wonderful support: Ralph Carter, Julie Conner, Connie Davis, Cara Elmen, Peter Haden, Joe Lepgold, and Kathy Schiff. My family members also deserve special credit, including my mother, Bettye Hobbs; sister, Linda McKinney; and aunt and uncle, Jane and Jack McPhaul. Finally, my husband, Steve Fishler, has stood by me through the thick and thin of it, and I give him my special thanks and love.

—Heidi H. Hobbs

1

"Think Globally, Act Locally"

The 1980s witnessed an unprecedented growth in grassroots activism on international issues. Interest groups frustrated at the national level during the Reagan and Bush administrations turned their efforts to the public. This public proved to be more attentive to the world around it as mass communication and modern transportation sharpened the public eye on events around the globe. Sensitized by the Vietnam era, international issues became a part of the political landscape by the end of the 1970s, with the hostage crisis in Iran and boycott of the 1980 Olympics. When the Reagan White House pulled away from the public in their conduct of foreign policy, activists took to the local communities and sounded the battle cry.

Local governments have been particularly responsive to the call and a target for much of this activism. As constituency demands and current lifestyles transcend city boundaries, the traditional roles exercised by the town leaders of America have grown in complexity. Municipal foreign policy in the United States has been the result of many factors: a more aware public; active interest groups frustrated at the national level turning to the cities; and the leadership of cities themselves, many of who came of age during the protests of the 1960s and now hold positions of power at the local level. The

1

result is that paving the streets and filling the potholes are often secondary to international agendas.

The majority of local contact with the world beyond has been cultural and diplomatic in nature, such as educational programs, artistic exchanges, and sister city relationships. Cultural interactions have proliferated in the post–World War II era with the advent of modern communication and the ease of international travel. They have included student exchange programs; international festivals; and art, music, dance, and theater delegations. Diplomatic actions have included visitors received (from formal consuls to tourists), missions abroad, and the development of relationships with cities in other countries. These pairings are often formed between cities with similar characteristics, such as port facilities or rural locations.

The more challenging phenomenon can be found in the economic and political realms. Economic actions are the fastest growing, most frequently characterized by cities seeking foreign trade and investment. Political issues, however, represent the greatest departure for cities as they venture beyond their traditional policy boundaries to make statements on more far-reaching issues, such as the apartheid regime in South Africa and political unrest in Central America.

Cultural and diplomatic relations can be thought of as a two-way street because they foster good relations from a humanitarian perspective that may also be used to develop economic and political relationships. This is particularly true of the sister cities program, which has frequently been used to develop both economic and political ties. For example, the joining of San Francisco and Shanghai was sought with an eye toward trade as former San Francisco mayor and current California senator Diane Feinstein actively courted the Chinese along with local businesspeople. The proliferation of sister city relationships with the former USSR during the cold war and Nicaragua while the United States was aiding the Contras, represent the more political side of these relationships. In both instances, sister city advocates believe their relationships were critical to the reversal of U.S. policy toward Nicaragua and facilitated the thawing of the cold war with the former Soviet Union.

The growth in economic activities can be explained by declining federal monies for cities and the need to generate independent sources of income. Economic contacts have been the most prolific and the most studied.[1] In addition to international trade and investment promotion, activities include trade missions to foreign countries, favorable zoning ordinances and local tax breaks for foreign investors, and port development. Cities are increasingly promoting foreign investment to offset the growing phenomenon of urban decay and local bankruptcy. Federal cutbacks coupled with an increasing budget deficit have forced cities to look elsewhere for financial backing, and international business interests have frequently been willing to fill the gap.

For example, when faced with the competition of low-cost foreign goods, the small textile community of Spartanburg, South Carolina, fought back.[2] Anticipating the decline of the textile industry, Spartanburg (population 45,800) actively sought foreign investment and has gained more than any other U.S. city its size. The city now hosts 60 firms from 12 countries, which represent an investment of more than $1 billion, and employs 7,000 area residents.

Political activities represent a new direction for cities. Using cultural, diplomatic, and economic interactions along with the more personal means afforded local politicians through their positions and access to the news media, cities have frequently taken contrary positions on key U.S. foreign policy initiatives. These actions have challenged federal supremacy in foreign policy. Four particularly controversial issues that represent this divergence include the comprehensive test ban movement, nuclear free zone declarations, divestment of local funds from South Africa, and provisions of sanctuary for Central American refugees.

All of these issues have generated not only a local focus but a national and international interest as well. Advocacy groups have vigorously promoted these activities and have seen a tremendous payoff in terms of resolutions passed. While the nuclear freeze movement was unable to pass a national resolution, it was successful in getting the support of more than 900 local communities. The comprehensive test ban movement grew out of the freeze movement's national shortcomings. Dissatisfied with federal responses to Soviet overtures for a comprehensive test ban, cities and counties across the United States began passing resolutions supporting a ban. By the end of the 1980s, resolutions had been passed by almost 200 local units. Activists behind the movement believe their activities were critical in the success of the 1987 Intermediate-Range Nuclear Forces (INF) Treaty.

Nuclear free zone declarations have also been an outgrowth of the nuclear free freeze movement, seeking to restrict the construction and transportation of nuclear materials in local communities. This not only has included the stationing and production of nuclear weapons but has been extended to power stations in some communities as well. As of December 1992, 157 municipalities, 32 counties, and one American Indian reservation had declared themselves a nuclear free zone.

Divestment grew out of a continuing concern with the apartheid political system of South Africa and dissatisfaction with official U.S. governmental response. The Reagan administration policy of constructive engagement was unacceptable to those who believed action against the apartheid regime was needed. To ensure a more direct response, activists went to the people for support. By the end of 1991, 101 cities and 25 counties had enacted some form of sanctions against South Africa.

Sanctuary for Central American refugees is a more sensitive issue as federal prosecution was particularly active and limited the number of localities willing to affiliate formally with the movement. The U.S. government's continued friendly relationship with the countries of El Salvador and Guatemala in the 1980s through periods of gross human rights violations spurred the movement onward and the desire to provide a sanctuary for refugees fleeing these countries. As of 1988, 28 cities and two states had adopted sanctuary resolutions.

The Bush administration reinforced many of the Reagan policies that had prompted local activism. These administrations were also operating in a political climate that encouraged local action on international issues. While not a policy objective, the Reagan administration initiated policies that provided a supportive climate for this behavior. First, the hard-line approach to foreign policy issues adopted by Reagan left many people dissatisfied with foreign policy administration. Reagan's ascension to power following Jimmy

Carter represented a radical departure in foreign policy for many of Carter's more liberal constituency. The Carter followers translated their feelings of helplessness at the polls into activism at the grassroots level where they could more easily access the reins of government. The activism and success of the nuclear freeze movement in gaining congressional attention in the early 1980s is indicative of this response.

Second, and perhaps more important, was the policy of new federalism. New federalism reinforced traditional Republican themes of reducing national government in favor of state and local responsibility for the provision of social services, education, and housing. President Bush supported this perspective with his call for volunteerism from a "thousand points of light." These policies, concurrent with the cutbacks on federal and local assistance funds and the promotion of free trade, pushed cities into the international arena economically.

But to be successful economically, cities had to build political relationships with their potential trade partners. This required greater contact abroad, a willingness to look internationally in economic development, encouragement of foreign investment, and acceptance of the emerging international division of labor that often disenfranchised the American work force. The effect was a new consciousness in international affairs that carried over to foreign policy concerns.

The Forces Behind the Issues

Political activism on international issues at the local level is not a mass movement. In actuality, the extent to which political issues, such as the comprehensive test ban, nuclear free zones, divestment and sanctuary, have become a part of local agendas is determined by the strength and influence of constituency demands, interest group activities, and local officials' response. The general public is particularly sensitive to international issues as constituency demands have been heightened by increasing global awareness at the local level. International events are vividly broadcast nightly

on televisions across America. The ability to communicate globally and travel with ease to worlds previously unknown has had a
profound effect on the issues brought to the national and subnational agenda. Often called the "CNN Revolution," the effects of
instantaneous transmittal of information cannot be ignored in
understanding these activities.

Perhaps more important, interest groups have been critical in
pushing international issues onto the local agenda as many of the
more controversial stands cities have taken have resulted from an
active lobby effort. Both national and local grassroots groups have
been involved in bringing foreign affairs to city hall. This is particularly true of the issues chosen for examination. These groups
have acted in two ways: seeking public awareness on a given issue
and securing alliances with local officials. Their ability to get the
general public's interest has often been helpful in forcing local
officials' hands.

Yet, the activities of interest groups are successful only to the
degree to which cities are responsive. The executive heads of city
government, mayors, have increasingly included foreign policy
issues in their campaign platforms and policy statements. While
mayors have long been active in the national policy process through
formal lobbying efforts, such as the U.S. Conference of Mayors
(USCM), they are currently expanding this role through more personal means. Capitalizing on a growing international consciousness, mayors have extended the powers of political office to participate in the foreign policy process. For example, both Mayor
David Dinkins of New York and former mayor of Los Angeles Tom
Bradley have used their offices to travel extensively. While these
trips are often taken to promote economic relationships, Mayor
Dinkins's trip to South Africa in November 1991 took on a political overtone as well, with Dinkins voicing support for continued
sanctions and speaking out on the political situation in that
country.[3]

Actions on international issues have often given mayors national
attention and resulted in political perks beyond city hall. In the
case of former San Antonio mayor Henry Cisneros, participation
on the bipartisan Kissinger Commission on U.S. activities in Central
America in the mid-1980s gained him national recognition that

later resulted in a Clinton cabinet appointment as secretary of housing and urban development.

While many officials have responded out of their personal beliefs, the case may also exist in which an official finds a statement or action on a given international issue to be politically expedient and responds accordingly. The argument can be made that many gestures are merely symbolic and designed to appease a local constituency without great sacrifice. For example, Mayor Richard M. Daley, Jr., of Chicago, along with representatives of eight other U.S. cities, participated in a conference call with Nelson Mandela of the African National Congress to address the increasing violence in South Africa in April 1991.[4] Following the call, Daley introduced a resolution to the Chicago Board of Aldermen that supported the call's discussions and established a victims of violence under apartheid fund. It passed one month later. There was little cost involved in the measure but the action gave Daley a stronger image in the anti-apartheid movement, which was of great concern to many of his constituents.

This example should not imply that mayors are without a conscience. Mark Allen, executive assistant to the former Berkeley mayor Eugene (Gus) Newport, believes that while the sensitivity of local officials to international issues are enhanced by the composition of their constituency and political expediency, there will always be "people of goodwill" who are sympathetic to and motivated by global concerns.[5] Many of the mayors who have moved on political issues have been motivated by a sincere desire to support an issue or cause. Most notably, black mayors like the former mayor Andrew Young of Atlanta and New York mayor David Dinkins have both been personally committed to the divestment campaigns undertaken in their cities and have often spoken on their behalf.

Much of the local success in international affairs has to do with the political dynamics of the cities involved. The operatives of local foreign policy are the governments of cities across the United States. What unites these cities in their foreign policy bids? It might be expected that the lingerings of 1960s radicalism would still have roots in Berkeley, California, or Boulder, Colorado, but Detroit, Michigan, does not fit this mold. Yet, more than 350 cities have acted on one or more of the issues targeted for investigation, encompassing 44 of the 50 states. Why have cities been targeted for these actions? Are there any commonalities that might motivate or reinforce their movement into international affairs?

Why Cities?

Several explanations for city involvement in foreign affairs can be offered. First and foremost, the international system has changed, and the way in which nations relate to one another is increasingly being redefined. Cities have become actors in this new environment. Second, the forces that govern cities have changed. New leadership has emerged from the social movements of the 1960s and 1970s to set far-reaching agendas for local governments. Finally, as urban development has proceeded, the cities themselves have changed. They are confronted with new challenges and opportunities either of little concern to them or that were previously handled by the federal government. Together these forces have combined to create an environment at the local level for international issues.

The debate in international relations today is concerned with the decline of the state in its ability to conduct foreign affairs and the growing network of nonstate actors in the international arena. While many authors have lined up on both sides of the fence, asserting the state's preeminence in foreign affairs[6] and suggesting there is a breakdown in the state's ability to cope with complex interactions,[7] there is consensus on the proliferation of nonstate actors in the international system pursuing their own foreign policy agenda.[8] If city activism is viewed in this context, it is one group of many actors who are seeking to get their views and agendas heard either in a traditional pluralist fashion, whereby the nation-state speaks with one voice in the international arena and represents the input of other actors critical to the policy formulation process, or in a broader capacity, communicating their message directly abroad. Both views are relevant to the issues examined here.

The decreased ability of the state to cope with complex issues has often resulted in public frustration with politics at the national level. Rosenau suggests there is a sense of fragmenting loyalties among citizens because of what they see as a lack of federal responsiveness to their concerns.[9] Feeling remote from the policy-making process, local leaders and their constituents are moved to act on international issues. Subgroups emerge around these issues as a result of an interested public, active interest groups, and sometimes simply vocal, interested individuals. The changing nature of the power structure at the local level coupled with this sense of alienation from the foreign policy process brings cities to the forefront as an outlet for the expression of the types of issues examined here.

A new leadership has emerged in cities that is receptive to these trends. Economic developments in the post–World War II era have prompted these changes, such that the growth strategies that propelled urban areas forward after the war experienced negative consequences by the 1970s. Redistributive policies, while often given lip service, were virtually nonexistent. The urban flight that promoted suburban development did not account for the disenfranchised, unemployed minorities that stayed behind in the urban centers.

Efforts to redress this situation have only made matters worse. Reclamation of urban areas has been carried out by and to the benefit of the prosperous. The service orientation of large urban areas has attracted a young, upper-middle-class professional and does not provide jobs for the poor. Local actions aimed at rebuilding a sense of community have resulted in gentrification of existing land holdings, in turn pushing up rents and further isolating the poor in substandard housing, if not sending them to the streets.

As a result of these developments, a new citizenry has come to dominate the politics of cities. The new urban dwellers came of age in the 1960s and now subscribe to many of the ideals and strategies imparted during those turbulent years. In many cities, a new consciousness has emerged, which challenges the status quo. Much of the pressure cities have had to bear, from declining federal assistance to growing crime, has required new and innovative policies to cope. A progressive response has emerged in many cities, which Kann has labeled "middle-class radicalism," a renewing of the leftist strategies so loudly espoused by students of the

1960s but with the middle-class assets of the 1980s.[10] Today, Kann argues, those calling for change have the power and resources available to them to make a difference. To develop his thesis, he points out the successes of the governing coalition in Santa Monica, California, in the early 1980s, led by the founder of Students for a Democratic Society (SDS) and now California state legislator from that district, Tom Hayden.

According to Kann, the core ideological drive of the Santa Monica left has been the creation of a "radical democracy."[11] Three concepts are central to this objective: creating a *human scale community*, based on *participatory democracy*, and a *one-class society*, which allows for personal gain, provided everyone enjoys a minimum level of economic self-sufficiency. While interpretation of these concepts has varied in practice, they are the essential cornerstones of middle-class radicalism as it has developed in Santa Monica. The greatest success of this movement has been the adoption of one of the strongest rent-control policies in the United States.

A similar argument is developed by Clavel for several localities across the United States.[12] Clavel identifies five cities—Hartford, Connecticut; Cleveland, Ohio; Berkeley and Santa Monica, California; and Burlington, Vermont—as the archetypal progressive cities of the 1980s. These cities have been characterized by a two-prong attack Clavel defines as focused on both "the legitimacy of absentee-owned and concentrated private power on the one hand, and on nonrepresentative city councils and city bureaucracies on the other." They have shifted their emphasis to public planning over private power, and "grass-roots citizen participation as an alternative to council-dominated representation."[13] The result is progressive government that has sought to develop a political system based on participation and not the "oligarchic rigidity of politics."[14]

These efforts have grown out of Lowi's contention that America had seen the "end of liberalism" by the 1970s, which most clearly manifested itself in local governing structures. It was here that special interests dominated and access to government was limited.[15] The response detailed by Kann and Clavel was a backlash against this stagnation.

Part of the reason cities have been fertile climates for citizen activism is because the foundations of liberalism, based on representation as a function of property rights, no longer exist in modern urban reality. In fact, Shefter notes that "by 1850, at the latest, a solid majority of the voters in large cities were proletarians in the strict sense of the term: they owned no property."[16] Efforts to ensure representation without property rights as a basis meant the public was often easier to ignore. To ensure representation required reevaluation and change in local governing structures. Such was the origins of the early reform efforts at the turn of the century and the emergence of the new progressivism of the 1970s and 1980s.

This perspective is reinforced by Pierce, Steger, Steel, and Lovrich who argue that increased citizen activism is a consequence of a postindustrial society, characterized by unprecedented affluence, a sense of security, and advanced technology and communication.[17] As a result, citizens have more time to involve themselves in diverse issues. Alger echoes these sentiments in his discussion of the increased international social consciousness of the middle class.[18] He believes this enhanced awareness stems from not only the people but their environment, particularly shifts in the global economy.

The geographical consequences of these developments as they affect the changing industrial base of the economy and localities are explored by Sawers and Tabb.[19] Declines in traditional industry resulted in shifts in production from the Northeast to the Sunbelt in the 1970s. Due to rising labor, land, and material costs, central city locations were no longer profitable. Clark suggests this movement was a function of not simply socioeconomic variables but decisions by political leaders removed from and insensitive to constituency demands.[20] The growth strategies pursued by local officials did not produce the necessary opportunities to maintain urban environments. The result was decaying urban centers with few prospects for their remaining populations.

To fight these trends, a citizen movement emerged in many cities that demanded city hall "do something." They sought to revitalize the political process, ensure democracy, and empower themselves in the local arena.[21] Traditionally, however, local governments have been unresponsive to public participation. The foundations of the reform movement in the late 1800s were based on the lack of public participation in city government.

The neo-Marxist/structuralist critique argues these goals were never realized, however, and the public remained disenfranchised from the governing process. Neo-Marxists believe the structure of government will always dominate the people at the citizen's expense. Even organized political action through interest groups has not gained the attention of local officials.[22] In some instances this position has led to disdain for organized community activities. The trials and tribulations of ACORN, a nationwide community organization that has represented low-income constituents, is a case in point.[23] Its activities have frequently met with local opposition in its efforts to improve the living standard for disenfranchised minorities.

Nevertheless, social movements have found an outlet at the local level. Their ability to set an agenda for city governments has enabled them to translate their issues into actions. Three ways in which environmental agendas that offer a method used in city activism may be set are proposed by Kamieniecki.[24]

Two of the models build from within the governmental structure: the inside-initiative and inside-access models, which are based on proximity and ability to influence the governmental process. The third, however—the outside-initiative model—suggests a public agenda may be sought first as a method for subsequent influence on traditional governmental action. This model is used to explain situations in which organizations outside of the governmental process are able to link their concerns with other organizations to get a place on the public agenda. These citizen organizations are then able to work together to put pressure on decision makers to adopt a formal agenda that will address their issues. Thus they have expanded the formal agenda through outside initiative. Kamieniecki is quick to note, however, that the success of this model is most likely in democratic societies, which are more receptive to diverse inputs.

In contrast to the adversarial position many local governments have taken toward community organizations, the new progressive movement has actively encouraged local activism. In seeking greater participation, local officials have opened themselves up to broader political demands. The result is not only a strengthening of national lobby efforts at the local level but the promotion of grassroots development as well.

Many of the same forces that have led to the establishment of more responsive local governments have also prompted actions on international issues. Progressive elements at the local level have brought international issues to the forefront in their push for greater government accountability. They have made great efforts to increase participation and local government responsiveness to community organizations. The new generation of leadership that found its voice in the protests of the 1960s is now in the position to bring about change in the local environment. Part of that change, due to increasing global interdependence, a shifting international political economy, and growing sensitivity to international concerns, is local activism on foreign affairs.

The interplay of these forces is exemplified in the issues identified here and local actions on them. Understanding of the international system has expanded to include a broad diversity of actors, of which cities are just a small part. Global public awareness is unavoidable in the modern age. The social consciousness of the 1960s has found a more formal way to express itself through subnational governmental entities. While activist groups remain committed to national lobbying, cities offer a willing ear and a positive and tangible forum for the expression of their interests. Finally, cities themselves have sought new ways to solve their problems, and while foreign policy has not always answered those issues, it has proved to be both a distraction and, in many instances, a crowd pleaser.

Local Politics and World Affairs

The growing problems of cities have generated an expanding awareness of the world around them. While it is easy to understand urban interest in foreign investment and trade development from a financial perspective, the following question remains: Why are cities acting on more discrete political issues? The issues targeted for investigation—the comprehensive test ban, nuclear free zones, divestment, and sanctuary—have limited returns for local entities. The initial assessment suggests city actions on these issues are a function of four forces: public opinion, interest groups, the characteristics of cities, and the system in which they operate. How might these forces be further explored?

Although there are limits to the effect public opinion may have on the policy process, it is the public who elects local officials and to whom the officials are responsible. On the four issues chosen for examination, the public has been very vocal. Public opinion polls have indicated that the general population is frequently in conflict with presidential policies, particularly in regard to the nuclear issues and divestment from South Africa. This trend challenges tradition-al wisdom that posits the chief executive as the "chief opinion maker," such that public opinion generally follows presidential initiatives in foreign affairs.[25] Turning to other outlets for the ex-pression of their concerns reinforces the debate on the nation-state's ability to cope with complex issues and may, in fact, sug-gest a fragmentation in national loyalties.[26]

To explain local governments' actions on international issues in terms of individuals and their opinions, however, is not complete. While the thesis may hold true that if the public disapproves of U.S. foreign policy goals, then it will find other outlets for expres-sion, such as cities, it is important to note the specialized nature of the constituency that supports international agendas. Previous studies indicate that it is the elite of the community, as defined by education and socioeconomic status, that is more likely to be concerned with international issues.[27]

Following this line of reasoning, the foci of response within the community must be clearly identified and the fragmentation thesis further expanded to examine the strengthened role of interest groups in American politics. Everson contends that three changes in American politics that suggest detachment from political in-stitutions—declines in the American public's confidence in the national government, political parties, and voter participation—have led to a fourth change, or "redirection of political energy into organized political activity," specifically an "increase in the role of interest groups in American politics."[28]

Interest groups have both fostered and taken advantage of these changing attitudes. Frequently frustrated in their attempts to influence national policy, they have tried a different approach by mobilizing support at the local level. The fact that interest groups have exercised a limited effect on local politics in the past may work to their advantage on international issues, as there is no precedent for their local involvement.[29] Information gathered from the groups themselves as well as their local representatives can identify their methods and ideology. The extent to which they are successful can be measured in terms of actions taken by cities on the issues.

Key to understanding the strength of public opinion and interest group activity is the distribution of power in local politics. How public opinion and interest group activity are used, if at all, in the decision-making process depends on the relative power they enjoy. Does public opinion count? Which interest groups have the ear of local politicians? Is the city structured in such a way to encourage or discourage local activism?

A central debate as to how power is distributed locally has been based on the conflict between elitist and pluralist interpretations of the local policy process. The elitist perspective views government as closed and the domain of the few, whereas the pluralist perspective, discussed earlier, suggests government processes diverse inputs to produce its final policy decisions. Numerous efforts have been made to examine which method is most represented and most responsive to public interests.[30]

An important impediment to identifying the sources of influence in the policy process has been the inability to draw significant correlations between actors and actions. To what extent are local actions on international issues a result of citizen activism? The persistence of influence from actors outside the policy process, i.e., the community, suggests there is some truth in the pluralist conception. The way in which this influence is assimilated, however, depends on the distribution of power in the decision-making process, supporting the elitist interpretation.

Bachrach and Baratz propose a theory of power assessment that encompasses these distinctions.[31] They suggest that power be measured not only in its most outward manifestations but also in terms of the bias that exists within the political system based on community norms and values. Are certain communities more likely to be open to local foreign policy initiatives? By knowing more about the cities themselves and their constituencies, some answers to these questions can be explored. U.S. Bureau of Census data are available on the characteristics of cities that have acted on the four issues. Are there underlying patterns that might categorize active cities based on these observations? Comparative data that include various demographic and economic variables for the populations of these localities can help in delineating the source of local support for the issues being addressed and the way in which power and influence are distributed within a given community.

The types of governing structures may also be critical to the way in which issues move through the system as they restrict or promote the types of inputs that successfully gain the attention of decision makers. For example, Lineberry and Sharkansky have found that unreformed city governments (characterized by the mayor-council system, partisan elections, and ward constituencies) are more likely to maximize the system's responsiveness to groups and interests in the population than reformed governments (characterized by a manager system, nonpartisan elections, and large constituencies).[32]

The relative strengths and weaknesses of mayors and councils may be critical in moving controversial issues into local politics. Studies show that the mayor has the greatest authority when he or she has been directly elected, has veto power, has a role in the budget process, has appointment powers, and serves a relatively long term in office.[33] In addition, the personal beliefs of key decision makers, their partisanship, their tenure in office, and their personal ambition may be important as well.

Also relevant is the role decision makers believe they should play. In terms of council members, studies suggest that most perceive their responsibility from a trustee perspective.[34] In other words, instead of acting as a delegate for a given area of constituents, officials believe they should act in a trustee role for their supporters and vote their conscience. Thus it is important to know something about the composition of the local governing structure in understanding local action on foreign policy issues.

In terms of the larger picture, the federal and international system, a reverse perspective must be employed. Traditionally, the study of cities has been concerned with the effects of federal policies on local governments. In contrast, this study is concerned with the effect of local policies on the system. Do local actions affect U.S. foreign policy either domestically, in terms of public acceptance, or in its impact abroad? Are the actions of cities diluting the effectiveness of U.S. foreign policy or undermining its objectives? What difference does it make if more than 100 cities have passed divestment legislation? Who is affected by these decisions: pension fund recipients whose savings are tied up in these investments, the apartheid regime of South Africa, South African blacks, congressional opponents, U.S. businesses operating in South Africa, or current U.S. foreign policy? What is the impact for these different groups and their interests?

The 1980s was the decade in which cities came of age as actors in the international arena and, more particularly, in the foreign policy process. The result of these activities in the 1990s is that cities have earned a new position as valid contenders in the policy process. This is particularly true in the economic realm as cities promote themselves internationally to attract foreign business. Political issues remain at the forefront as well, however, as the traditional forums for local international contact, such as Sister Cities International, are no longer singularly focused on efforts to promote friendly relations between nations and solidify the cold war world. Instead, the relationships are more concerned with favorable trade relations, export-import promotion, and political and social development.

To understand how these structures operate today in regard to local activism on foreign policy, the following chapters offer an overview of the issues targeted for investigation, public opinion on those issues, and interest group activities as they developed in the 1980s. A profile of active cities and their constituents, using census data, is then put forth, followed by a review of federal and international limitations to these actions. Finally, the future of municipal foreign policy is addressed. In what direction will cities head in the 1990s? Whither municipal foreign policy?

Notes

1. A good overview of these activities is provided in Fry, E. H., Radebaugh, L. H., & Soldatos, P. (Eds.). (1989). *The new international cities era: The global activities of North American municipal governments.* Provo, UT: Brigham Young University.

2. Treadwell, D. (1985, October 27). South Carolina mill town weaves a new economy. *Los Angeles Times,* sec. 1, p. 1.

3. Purudm, T. S. (1991, November 18). Dinkins, in South Africa, widens economic efforts: Leaves without meeting with top officials. *New York Times,* sec. B, p. 3.

4. Mandela calling. (1992, Spring-Summer). *Global Communities, A Newsletter of the Institute for Policy Studies,* p. 6.

5. Interview with Mark Allen, Berkeley, California, July 22, 1985.

6. See, for example, Evans, P., Rueschmeyer, D., & Skocpol, T. (Eds.). (1985). *Bringing the state back in.* Cambridge: Bambirdge University Press; Krasner, S. (1984). Approaches to the state: Alternative conceptions and historical dynamics. *Comparative Politics, 16,* 223-246; and Waltz, K. (1979). *Theory of international politics.* New York: Random House.

7. See, for example, Ferguson, Y. H., & Mansbach, R. W. (1989). *The state, conceptual chaos, and the future of international relations theory* (GSIS Monograph Series in World Affairs). Boulder, CO: Rienner; and Rosenau, J. N. (1988). The state in an era of cascading politics: Wavering concept, widening competence, withering colossus, or weathering change? *Comparative Political Studies, 21,* 19-30.

8. A good general discussion of these issues can be found in Hobbs, H. (1992, March-April). *New actors and alternate views of the foreign policy process.* Paper presented at the 33rd annual covention of the International Studies Association, Atlanta, GA.

9. Rosenau, J. N. (1984, September). A pre-theory revisited: World politics in an era of cascading interdependence. *International Studies Quarterly, 28,* 245-305.

10. Kann, M. E. (1986). *Middle class radicalism in Santa Monica.* Philadelphia: Temple University Press.

11. Kann (1986).

12. Clavel, P. (1986). *The progressive city: Planning and participation, 1969-1984.* New Brunswick, NJ: Rutgers University Press.

13. Both quotes from Clavel (1986, p. 1).

14. Clavel (1986, p. 232).

15. Lowi, T. *The end of liberalism: The second republic of the United States* (2nd ed.). New York: Norton.

16. Shefter, M. (1984). Images on the city in political science: Communities, administrative entities, competitive markets, and seats of chaos. In L. Rodwin & R. M. Hollister (Eds.), *Cities of the mind: Images and themes of the city in the social sciences* (pp. 55-82). New York: Plenum Press. (Quote from p. 81.)

17. Pierce, J. C., Steger, M. A. E., Steel, B. S., & Lovrich, N. P. (1992). *Citizens, political communication, and interest groups.* Westport, CT: Praeger.

18. Alger, C. F. (1990). The world relations of cities: Closing the gap between social science paradigms and everyday human experience. *International Studies Quarterly, 34,* 493-518.

19. Sawers, L., & Tabb, W. K. (Eds.). (1984). *Sunbelt/Snowbelt: Urban development and regional restructuring.* New York: Oxford University Press.

20. Clark, T. N. (1985). Fiscal strain: How different are Snow Belt and Sun Belt cities? In P. E. Peterson (Ed.), *The new urban reality* (pp. 253-280). Washington, DC: Brookings Institution.

21. Berry, J. M., Portney, K. E., & Thomson, K. (1993). *The rebirth of urban democracy.* Washington, DC: Brookings Institution.

22. Peterson, P. E. (1981). *City limits.* Chicago: University of Chicago Press.

23. Delgado, G. (1986). *Organizing the movement: The roots and growth of ACORN.* Philadelphia: Temple University Press.

24. Kamieniecki, S. (1991). Political mobilization, agenda building and international environmental policy. *Journal of International Affairs, 44*(2), 339-358.

25. Mueller, J. E. (1973). *War, presidents and public opinion.* New York: Wiley.

26. Rosenau (1984).

27. Hughes, B. B. (1978). *The domestic context of American foreign policy.* San Francisco: Freeman. See also Wittkopf, E. R. (1987, June). Elites and masses: Another look at attitudes toward America's world role. *International Studies Quarterly, 31,* 131-159.

28. Everson, D. H. (1982). *Public opinion and interest groups in American politics.* New York: Franklin Watts. (Quote from pp. 88-89.)

29. Peterson (1981).

30. Hahn and Levine offer a good discussion of these perspectives in the introduction to their edited volume. Hahn, H., & Levine, C. H. (Eds.). (1984). *Readings in urban politics: Past, present, and future* (2nd ed.). New York: Longman.

31. Bachrach, P., & Baratz, M. S. (1984). Two faces of power. In H. Hahn & C. H. Levine (Eds.), *Readings in urban politics: Past, present, and future* (2nd ed., pp. 149-158). New York: Longman.

32. Lineberry, R. L., & Sharkansky, I. (1978). *Urban politics and public policy* (3rd ed.). New York: Harper & Row.

33. Lineberry & Sharkansky (1978).

34. Lineberry & Sharkansky (1978).

2

Changing Latitudes:
International Issues
and Public Response

The political issues that cities have acted on are diverse, as illustrated by the four chosen for examination: comprehensive test ban, nuclear free zone, divestment, and sanctuary. Each has its own unique history and specialized constituency. Although public opinion has broadened on these issues, much of the expanded awareness has been due to the interest groups that promoted them. The comprehensive test ban and nuclear free zone declarations grew out of the nuclear freeze activities of the early 1980s. Divestment has been an ongoing movement for several years, starting in the religious and academic communities. Similarly, the sanctuary movement grew out of a religious orientation, involving cities only in the latter part of the 1980s. A more detailed history of their development demonstrates the close relationship that emerged between the public and activists on these issues to move cities into action in the 1980s.

Nuclear Politics

The fear of conflict that exists in the nuclear age has been one of the most pronounced aspects of public convergence on a foreign policy issue. Woodrow Wilson's hope that World War I would be "the war to end all wars" became a potential reality in the face of nuclear weapons. If a third world war were to occur, a nuclear conflict *could be* the war to end all wars with its capacity to eradicate human civilization as it presently exists. The fear of such an eventuality has prompted public outbursts in response to what many have felt to be shortsighted national leadership. The failure of SALT II during the Carter administration, the unwillingness of the Reagan administration to support a nuclear test ban treaty, and the development of the Strategic Defense Initiative (SDI) are but a few trends that have fanned these fears. Even with the break up of the USSR and ongoing negotiations toward the elimination of nuclear weapons, their continued existence remains a fearful specter.

In response to these concerns, citizens banded together and interest groups formed to promote a freeze on the production of nuclear weapons in the 1980s. The movement traces its beginnings to a paper written by Randall Foresberg (1979), director of the Institute for Defense and Disarmament Studies, titled "The Call to Halt the Nuclear Arms Race."[1] Response was overwhelming to this paper, with national organizations, regional and local groups, and individuals endorsing the freeze proposal. Since that time, citizens across the United States have supported some form of nuclear freeze, either through town meetings, local referenda, resolutions, or initiatives. The results are staggering: More than 900 local governments have acted on the freeze issue.[2]

Public opinion on the question of nuclear armaments has been clear and consistent. In one of the first Gallup Polls using the freeze language, 71% of the respondents favored an agreement between the United States and USSR for "an immediate, verifiable freeze in the testing and production of nuclear weapons."[3] Opposition was registered by only 20% of the sample, with 9% having no opinion. Similar figures were obtained in 1984, with freeze support showing a 7% increase as 78% of the respondents favored a freeze, 18% opposed, and only 4% had no opinion.[4]

A Harris survey poll in 1984 also found 78% support for a House of Representatives bill that would call for the United States to negotiate "a verifiable nuclear freeze agreement with the Soviet Union."[5] Even following the failure of the Geneva arms talks, the Harris poll still found that 90% of those surveyed in July 1984 favored the United States and USSR sitting down to negotiate an agreement to reduce nuclear weapons.[6] An agreement to ban all underground testing of nuclear weapons was favored by 80%.

Action on nuclear issues has been initiated by interest groups disenchanted with their limited influence in the national arena seeking outlets of expression at the grassroots level. Their inability to bring about meaningful change at the national level has prompted activism at more accessible levels of the governing structure. Local governments have offered a legitimate avenue through which these views may be expressed. The national organization that has coordinated much of this movement is the Nuclear Weapons Freeze Campaign (NWFC). Founded in 1981, the NWFC has connected more than 1,400 groups across the United States and has had state- based offices in all 50 states. The group has served as an international contact point for freeze/peace groups from around the world. Nationally, its activities have ranged from congressional lobbying to the coordination and staffing of an annual conference in which freeze delegates elected from congressional districts across the country participate.[7]

The efforts of freeze advocates brought the issues into national focus in 1981-1982, resulting in congressional debate on the possibility of a nuclear freeze resolution. The inability of the freeze movement to get a national resolution passed broadened the outlets of influence sought. The freeze campaign expanded to include other means to halt the arms race, including local initiatives. The language that developed around this movement is one of "peace and justice." Other national groups critical to this movement in the 1980s included the following organizations:

Washington Peace Center
Coalition for a New Foreign and Military Policy

Local Elected Officials of America for Social Responsibility
Center for Economic Conversion
National Center for Policy Alternatives
SANE: Committee for a Sane Nuclear Policy

Local freeze groups at both the state and city/county levels also formed to make their presence known. Their effectiveness has been limited, however, due to the proliferation of organizations frequently working without coordination of effort and often operating at cross-purposes. Recognizing these limitations, the NWFC merged with SANE in 1987 to consolidate forces and facilitate coordination of activities.

According to Larry Agran, former director of the Local Elected Officials of America for Social Responsibility (LEO-SR), much of the local action was a response to the increasing military budget, which prevented the provision of many local social services.[8] Agran believes citizens have an "abiding sense of frustration" with the formulation and implementation of foreign policy. For many citizens, the escalating military budget suggests foreign policy is another name for military spending. In a *Los Angeles Times* editorial Agran argued:

> The plain and indisputable truth is that the more than $290 billion that our federal government is spending annually for military purposes is robbing our people, and our cities and towns, of the resources to sustain personal well-being, economic prosperity and social progress.[9]

To alter this situation, the objective of LEO-SR was to establish a national network that could serve as a basis for orchestrating a shift in American foreign policy out of the arms race and into addressing local concerns. Toward this end, the group sought the adoption of the Main Street Economic Agenda, which advocated the transfer of expenditures from the military to more productive domestic enterprises, channeling the funds into increased revenue sharing for local entities.

In 1986, the Local Elected Officials project joined with the Center for Innovative Diplomacy (CID), a nonprofit, citizen-based organization aimed at the development of municipal foreign policy. Michael Shuman, a founder of CID, served as the president of CID, while Agran assumed the title of executive director for the CID/ LEO merger. With the merger came the publication of the best summary of local activities on international issues, *The Bulletin of Municipal Foreign Policy*. Published quarterly, this bulletin provided reprints of articles on local activism from around the United States, updates on current activities, and commentary on the articles and issues by CID/LEO officials. Unfortunately, it ceased publication in 1991.

The comprehensive test ban movement represents one of the more recent outgrowths of the freeze organizations. The effort was fueled by the USSR moratorium on testing, which began on August 6, 1985 (the commemoration day of the bombing of Hiroshima). Despite this overture, the United States continued testing, and subsequently, the Soviets resumed as well. The test ban movement continued to be very active, however, with activists staging protests at all test sites and urging localities to pass resolutions supporting the ban. Almost 200 cities and 20 counties had passed nonbinding resolutions supporting the ban by the end of the 1980s.

One of the more significant successes of this effort took place on December 13, 1987, at the Nevada Nuclear Weapons Test Site.[10] The protest grew out of the success of "The Nevada Declaration," a statement signed by more than 700 local elected officials that called for an end to the arms race and a redirection of resources to U.S. cities. The protest was staged to coincide with the 64th Congress of the National League of Cities meeting in Las Vegas, Nevada. The participation of several local officials strengthened the protest. According to Maggie Murphy, a SANE/Freeze organizer for Westside Los Angeles:

> There were many people I'd seen before at the test site. And though they'd never taken civil disobedience before, they did this time because of the city officials. The participation of city officials was inspiring. Their presence really lent the action a lot of credibility.[11]

Over the next few years, several actions were taken in Congress to support these efforts. A resolution supporting negotiations toward a ban and urging ratification of the Threshold Test Ban and Peaceful Explosion Treaty was passed by the House in February

1986.[12] The following year, Senators Edward Kennedy (D-MA), Alan Cranston (D-CA), and Mark Hatfield (R-OR) all sought to introduce legislation supporting the ban but withdrew their proposals to facilitate summit negotiations on the INF treaty.[13]

The test ban concept is not new. The first such treaty, the Partial Test Ban Treaty, was signed in 1963 by the United States, the USSR, and the UK to move all testing underground. Although intended as a step toward limiting testing, the treaty has not slowed the rate of testing, and in actuality, it has served as little more than an anti-air pollution measure.[14] In recent years, nonnuclear signatories to the treaty have sought to reopen it to amendments to move toward a comprehensive ban. The United States, the UK, and France voted against this action, but under provisions of the treaty, they may be forced to be a part of a conference, if convened, to consider amendments.[15]

To mark the 25th anniversary of this treaty, SANE/Freeze activists, along with Parliamentarians Global Action and International Physicians for the Prevention of Nuclear War, held ceremonies in cities across the United States in 1988.[16] They declared August 5 to be International Test Ban Day and organized activities across the United States to coincide with commemoration of the Hiroshima/ Nagasaki bombings on Hiroshima Day, August 6. According to Tonkavitch, the commemoration represented an effort to bring the comprehensive test ban movement home.[17] Previously, the tactics of the movement had revolved around protests at test sites. These activities were directed at generating local awareness through demonstrations, workshops, and teach-ins.

Despite both the Reagan and Bush administrations' unwillingness to support a test ban, public response has been favorable. A supportive public has lent both credibility and strength to the activities of the movement and has been critical to the successes at the local level. Specifically, in April 1986, the Gallup Poll posed the following question:

> The Soviet Union has had a ban on underground tests of nuclear weapons since last August. The U.S. has rejected such a ban and has conducted eight underground tests since then. The Reagan administration argues that these tests are necessary to develop new weapons

and to assure the reliability of existing weapons. Do you think the
U.S. should or should not agree to a ban on nuclear testing if the Soviet
Union continues their ban?[18]

Of those interviewed, 56% felt the United States should agree to
such a ban, 35% felt that United States should not agree, and 9%
had no opinion. The greatest support was found among college
graduates, with 65% supportive, 31% opposed, and 4% with no
opinion.[19] Regionally, the South was most divided on the issue,
with 44% supportive, 42% opposed, and 14% with no opinion. In
the other regions of the country—East, Midwest, and West—support ranged between 61% and 63%.

In a survey conducted almost one year later in March 1987, similar
views were expressed.[20] In response to this statement "Further
increases and improvements in nuclear weapons would not give
either the U.S. or the Soviet Union a real advantage over the other,"
69% agreed, 21% disagreed, and 10% had no opinion. Continued
fear of the results of a nuclear conflict were also expressed in
response to the following statement: "There would be no winner
in an all-out nuclear war; both the U.S. and the Soviet Union would
be completely destroyed." Of those surveyed, 83% agreed with
this statement, 10% disagreed, and 7% had no opinion. Toward
addressing this fear and slowing down the arms race, support for
the Intermediate Nuclear Forces Treaty one week before its sign-
ing was overwhelming with 76% approving the treaty, 13% disapproving, and 11% with no opinion.[21]

Arising from similar concerns but coming from a somewhat
different perspective is the establishment of nuclear free zones
(NFZs) across the United States. The objective of nuclear free zone
designations, according to the Nuclear Free Zone Registry,[22] is
"the prohibition of all development, testing, transportation,
deployment, funding and usage of nuclear weapons within designated borders." The movement grew out of the NWFC's failure to
obtain a national commitment. Its historical tradition is based on
international treaties that have designated Antarctica (1959),
outer space (1967), Latin America (1967), and the seabed (1971)
as NFZ territories. Both the United States and the USSR were
signatories to these agreements.

The first U.S. city to declare itself a nuclear free zone was Garrett Park, Maryland, in 1982.[23] Since that time, the movement has grown to almost 200 cities and counties as of December 1992. Globally, there are more than 4,533 nuclear free zones in 25 countries. It is important to note that not all of the local declarations have been legally binding. A local ordinance or charter amendment is required as opposed to a city resolution. According to the Nuclear Free America, a clearinghouse and resource center for nuclear free zones, almost 100 cities and counties had passed legally binding ordinances by the end of 1992.

While public opinion polls have not addressed the question of nuclear free zones, they have examined public support for nuclear power plant construction, which is opposed by the free zone advocates. The Harris survey has asked the following question since 1975 in regard to nuclear power: "In general, do you favor or oppose the building of more nuclear power plants in the United States?"[24] In March 1975, following the energy crisis of 1973-1974, 63% favored increased construction, while 19% were opposed and 18% were not sure. This trend of support began to decline over the next few years until May 1980 when the opposition pulled ahead with 49% compared with 39% in favor of increased construction and 12% still not sure. By December 1988, opposition had increased to 61%, with only 30% in favor and the number of those unsure decreased to 9%.

Other actions taken on nuclear issues in the 1980s included the rejection of nuclear shelter plans, the formation of the Jobs for Peace Campaign and local peace budgets, the development of ties with Soviet sister cities, and the establishment of local peace commissions. Since 1981, following the lead of Cambridge, Massachusetts, more than 100 cities voted to reject the Federal Emergency Management Agency's (FEMA) efforts to institute Crises Relocation Planning (nuclear shelters) for local entities. More than 80 localities responded to the Jobs for Peace Campaign, which sought the passage of local ordinances requiring city governments to publish annual reports documenting the impact of U.S. military spending on the community. This movement included cities such as Los Angeles and San Jose, California, whose economies depend heavily on military contracts.

The objective of the Soviet sister city program was to develop informal ties that could lead to future cooperation. This movement snowballed toward the end of the 1980s with the advent of glasnost and perestroika under Gorbachev. In addition, there were at least three peace commissions established at the local level—Washington, D.C.; Cambridge, Massachusetts; and Boulder, Colorado. According to Brugmann, former director of the Cambridge [Massachusetts] Peace Commission, Cambridge was the first city to create "a municipal peace department, and still has the most extensive example of such an agency."[25] The primary function of such entities was the promotion of local government peace advocacy, such as adopting some of the programs detailed above.

U.S. Policy Toward South Africa

In a more direct manner, the growing international concern with South Africa has demonstrated the heightened awareness of individuals to the world around them. The inequities perpetuated by the apartheid regime of South Africa gained greater global attention in the 1980s as the majority black population (75%) raised their voices in opposition to the ruling white minority (14%). Prominent black South Africans, such as Bishop Desmond Tutu and formerly jailed African National Congress (ANC) leader Nelson Mandela and his wife, Winnie Mandela, have given their support to opposition efforts and urged other countries to join the struggle.

During the 1980s, the United States was reticent to break its lucrative financial ties with South Africa, and many U.S. based businesses continued to operate in that country. Underlying this economic incentive was a more strategic concern, as many believed that divestment would weaken the U.S. position in South Africa and its ability to influence events in that country. In an attempt to pacify activists on these issues, many businesses and academic institutions adopted the Sullivan principles, a code of conduct designed to ensure greater equality and opportunity for blacks in foreign-owned businesses. Opposition activists claimed this was not enough, however, and did little more than tacitly recognize the existing problems. They believed stronger actions must be taken to let the South African government know their institutionalized racist form of government could not exist. A major outgrowth of this concern was the Campaign Against Investment in South Africa (CAISA).

CAISA was a coalition of organizations devoted to ending the apartheid practices of South Africa and more specifically, to divest state and local funds from companies doing business there. The following organizations were all a part of this effort and continue to support its basic mission of bringing about change in South Africa:

American Committee on Africa
American Friends Service Committee
Clergy and Laity Concerned
Connecticut Anti-Apartheid Committee
Interfaith Center on Corporate Responsibility
TransAfrica
United Nations Methodist Office
Washington Office on Africa

Beyond disdain for the repressive practices of the South African government as justification for their concern, CAISA argued that the United States was providing "vital economic, political and military support to the minority regime" during the Reagan administration.[26] Corporate involvement included oil imports, transportation manufacturing, and computer assistance.

Reinforcing this point, President Reagan supported continued involvement of U.S. corporations in South Africa based on the argument that "constructive engagement" would bring about "quiet diplomacy."[27] The administration contended that significant changes were occurring within the country that would give greater representation to nonwhites. Therefore, it was best to maintain relations at status quo. Toward this end, export controls implemented under the Carter administration were eased to allow strategic materials such as planes, helicopters, and computer technology to be exported to South Africa for "civilian use."

CAISA's position was upheld when the president's policy suffered a major setback as a high-level task force mandated by Secretary of State George Shultz to review the policy of constructive engagement found it to be ineffective.[28] Calling for stronger economic actions, the fairly conservative committee, which consisted of several major U.S. industry representatives, former government officials, lawyers, and academics, condemned the tolerance the administration had shown toward the repressive practices of the South African government. These findings not only sustained but supported the 1986 congressional overturn of the president's sanctions legislation veto.

In international forums as well, the United States continued tacitly to support the South African regime. The U.N. Security Council veto by the United States and the UK of a proposal to impose U.N. economic sanctions against South Africa (in February 1987) reiterated the president's opposition to the imposition of economic actions against South Africa.[29] This position was maintained despite public outcry and congressional action to the contrary.

Local actions grew out of public opinion dissatisfied with the Reagan administration's leadership on South Africa. In August 1985, the Gallup Poll found public support very divided on the way President Reagan was handling the South African situation.[30] Of the total sample, 35% approved of the president, 32% disapproved and 33% has no opinion. Of a more informed sample determined by knowledge of the issue, 40% approved, 44% disapproved, and 16% had no opinion. Later that year (October 1985), of the total sample, the presidential approval rate had dropped to 33% and disapproval had risen to 39%.[31] Of an aware group also surveyed at that time, 47% of those polled wanted more pressure exerted by the U.S. government on South Africa, 15% called for less pressure, 30% favored the same, and 8% had no opinion. Breakdown by racial groups found 74% black and nonwhite respondents wanted more pressure compared with 42% white.

In the following year (September 1986), the Gallup Poll again looked at public support for U.S. pressure on the South African government to end apartheid.[32] Asked of the 58% who said they had followed South African events closely, support for more pressure had grown by 8% to 55%; 14% called for less pressure. Those who favored the same amount of pressure had decreased by 6% to 24%, while those with no opinion stayed about the same at 7%.

In the same survey, the aware group was asked whether the United States should or should not apply tougher economic sanctions, such as a trade embargo or ending U.S. investment in South Africa.[33] In response, 53% felt the United States should apply tougher sanctions, 34% were against, and 13% had no opinion. Breakdowns of the poll found Democrats favoring tougher sanctions over the Republicans, 62% to 46%. Similar support came from nonwhites, with 74% favoring tougher sanctions; 63% of the young (18- to 29-year-olds) were in favor compared with 46% in the over 50 sample.

Comparable results were reported in a Harris survey conducted in January 1985: 68% of those polled favored pressure on the South African government, 21% opposed, and 11% were not sure.[34] By July 1986, support for pressure had increased to 78%, opposition had decreased to 16%, and only 6% were not sure.[35] The 1985 survey also asked about protests going on at that time outside the South African Embassy in Washington, D.C., and consulates in other cities and found 63% were sympathetic with the protests, 28% unsympathetic, and 9% neither or not sure.

Supporting growing citizen awareness of this issue were changing responses to the question of U.S. businesses operating in South Africa, a critical concern of the divestment movement. Respondents were asked whether they favored or opposed the use of these businesses to put pressure on the South African government. In November 1976, 46% favored business actions, 28% opposed them, and 26% were not sure. By January 1985, 70% favored business pressure, 24% opposed, and only 6% were not sure.[36]

Specifically, two types of business pressure were examined by Harris in 1985 and 1986. In response to the proposal of preventing all new U.S. business investment in South Africa, 52% were in favor, 42% were opposed, and 6% were not sure in July 1986 compared with 48% in favor, 47% opposed, and 5% not sure in January 1985.[37] More dramatically, in response to the question of whether all U.S. businesses now in South Africa should be forced to close their operations, 36% were in favor in July 1986 compared with

18% in January 1985. Opposition decreased from 76% in 1985 to 60% in 1986, with 6% not sure in 1985 as opposed to 4% in 1986.

The Harris survey in July 1986 also addressed how the Reagan administration had handled the problem of putting pressure on the government of South Africa to end its apartheid policy.[38] Only 36% of those surveyed felt the administration was doing a pretty good to excellent job, whereas 60% felt the administration's handling was only fair to poor and 4% were not sure. Later that year, following the congressional override of the president's sanctions legislation veto, the Harris survey found support for the congressional action among 54% of those polled, with 32% who thought it was not right and 14% who were not sure.[39]

The Bush administration did not fare much better with the public on the question of South Africa. By 1990, public opinion polls found increased support for the maintenance of sanctions toward South Africa, despite the president's leaning toward lifting them. Specifically, the Harris survey found 66% favored continued use of sanctions, with 27% opposed and 7% not sure.[40] Almost identical results were reported by the Gallup (1991) poll.

Why Divest?

Proponents argued divestment at the state and local levels was one of the most effective ways to discourage the continued operation of U.S. businesses in South Africa. Initial divestment efforts in the 1960s targeted the businesses themselves through shareholder consciousness, universities, and churches that were urged to withdraw their investments from banks making loans to and withholdings in South Africa.[41] While state and local governments were targeted in the early 1970s, it was not until the 1980s, with the growing discontent in South Africa and the imposition of a state of emergency in that country prompting international public condemnation, that actions were taken.

The rationale to involve state and local governments was based on the amount of money involved. By 1988, there were 23 states, 14 counties, and more than 70 cities that had passed divestment actions, and the numbers have grown since that time. Together they accounted for approximately $19.6 billion in public funds that had been redirected away from firms that do business in or with South Africa.[42] These actions were primarily aimed at pension holdings. CAISA provided interested parties with a packet of materials that included a guide on how to solicit local support for divestment initiatives.

The movement to involve states and cities also brought the discussion of South Africa into local policy arenas, which heightened attention not only locally but, it was hoped, at the national level as well. Through divestment, the proponents argued, the economic power of both corporate investors and the pension funds of localities would be brought to bear on institutions doing business in South Africa and thus precipitate their withdrawal. It was hoped that this withdrawal and subsequent governmental pressure would bring about changes in that country.

Central America
and the Sanctuary Movement

Much in the way Vietnam and Southeast Asia came into American homes during the 1960s and 1970s, Central America become a new part of the map for U.S. citizens in the 1980s. Honduras, Costa Rica, Panama, and most important, Nicaragua became geographical points of reference on television screens across America. Many objections have been raised to U.S. involvement in Central America, particularly the Reagan administration policy to support the Contra rebels in their attempts to overthrow the Sandinista government of Nicaragua.

The denial of human rights and the roaming death squads in El Salvador and Guatemala came to the attention of U.S. citizens through efforts made by refugees, their sanctuary hosts, and activist groups like Amnesty International and Para los Niños. While local actions were not as official and did not have the impact of other actions such as divestment, cities did take a stand on Central America through public statements, nonbinding resolutions, and less formal ceremonial ties and affiliations to express their dissatisfaction with the state of relations with those countries.

Some of the efforts undertaken by local actors included the development of sister city relationships with cities in Nicaragua (87 cities and states had relationships by the end of the 1980s), nonbinding resolutions that protested U.S. policy in Central America (San Francisco, Seattle, and Boulder were among the first), expressions of friendship and goodwill, and the solicitation for assistance funds by local officials for humanitarian objectives. For the most part, these actions proceeded without invoking the legitimacy of city hall in the transactions; however, local elected officials were very active in these activities. Examples range from citizens in Burlington, Vermont, arranging for a ship to take 560 tons of human- itarian goods, including 30 tons of medical supplies, to its sister city Puerto Cabezas, Nicaragua,[43] to Boulder, Colorado, undertaking the construction of a preschool in its friendship city Jalapa, Nicaragua. Completed in 1986, the Jalapa school was built through money raised by a campaign fund chaired by Homer Page, a city councilman of Boulder. While the council did not formally sanction the fund raising, it did authorize a friendship pact with the city. Page described the venture as a "people to people" effort and not for or against administration policy.[44]

The continuing conflict in Central America brought U.S. mayors together in support of the Central American Peace Plan put forth by Costa Rican president Oscar Arias to bring peace to the region. In a declaration issued at the January 1988 meeting of the U.S. Conference of Mayors in Washington, D.C., 39 mayors pledged their support for the peace plan.[45] The mayors' movement grew in response to the Reagan administration's lukewarm support for the plan and continued provision of aid to the Contras. Their view was backed by public opinion, with the Gallup Poll finding 67% of those surveyed believing the United States should support the plan.[46]

The Reagan administration's decision to support the Contra rebels in Nicaragua against the Sandinista government was generally *not* supported by public opinion. Following the March 1, 1985, decision to step up support for the Contras, the Gallup Poll found a 46% disapproval rate on how the president was handling the situation in Nicaragua; 26% approved and 31% had no opinion.[47] Similar results were reported in August 1986 before the Iran-Contra deal had fully come to light, with 34% approving the president's handling of the problem, 46% disapproving, and 20% with no opinion.[48] The following year (in September 1987) just after the Iran- Contra hearings, results were somewhat different, with the approval rating dropping seven points to 27%, disapproval increased to 58%, and 15% had no opinion.[49] Not surprisingly, Democrats' disapproval rate was a large 78% compared with 41% by the Republicans.

This trend continued as the 1988 presidential election approached. The public generally approved of the way in which President Reagan was handling his job: 51% to 35%, with 14% of no opinion.[50] The approval rating for foreign policy was also good at 54%, with 35% disapproval and 11% with no opinion. The figures were quite different, however, in regard to Central American issues, specifically what the poll described as the "situation in Nicaragua" and the "situation in Panama." The disapproval rating for Nicaragua was 55% (26% approved and 19% had no opinion), whereas the disapproval rate for Panama was 53% (27% approved and 20% had no opinion).

The prospects for Bush after the election were not much better in this area: Of those surveyed, only 16% thought Bush would do a better job in either Nicaragua or Panama. The majority, 46% in the Nicaragua case and 50% in Panama, believed Bush would do about the same. Skeptics in both cases who thought Bush would not do as good constituted 21%.

Some of the national groups devoted to enhancing U.S. understanding of Central America during the 1980s included the following organizations:

Central America Resource Center
Chicago Religious Task Force on Central America
Neighbor to Neighbor Education Fund
U.S. Out of Central America

The primary function of these groups was information sharing. In addition, the Central America Resource Center ran the Refugee

Legal Support Service,[51] which provided refugee defense lawyers
with documentation for political asylum cases involving Central
American refugees.

Although Nicaragua was at the center of attention, given
administration priorities at this time, a growing concern emerged
around the plight of refugees from Central America. The case of
sanctuary provision for Central American refugees represented
the greatest challenge to federal authority of the issues considered
here. More than 20 cities and two states declared themselves
sanctuaries for Central American refugees who were fleeing
political persecution in their countries.

Primarily, the requests for sanctuary came from Salvadoran and
Guatemalan refugees. The U.S. government, however, has traditionally been friendly with the governments of these countries and
did not consider the refugees' flight one of freedom from political
oppression. Rather, the government argued—most notably, the
Immigration and Naturalization Service (INS)—that they were economic refugees seeking better financial conditions. Meanwhile,
in both countries, opposition to the U.S. supported government
administrations resulted in thousands of civilian deaths. Death
squads roamed the countryside both in opposition to the government and in support of radical factions.

The sanctuary movement bases its historical foundations on the
traditional Judeo-Christian/Greek concept that the church would
provide sanctuary for "believers" fleeing persecution. The underground railroad of the Civil War was undertaken in this tradition.[52]
A more modern application occurred in 1971 when the city of
Berkeley declared itself a refuge for sailors on board the *USS Coral
Sea,* an aircraft carrier, seeking asylum from the Vietnam War.
Sanctuary was provided in the University Lutheran Church. The
city was instrumental in arranging bail for the sailors and negotiat-
ing conscientious observer status for them.

The present movement grew in protest to the trial of 11 clergy-
men and lay workers in Tucson, Arizona, who in 1986 where accused
of smuggling illegal aliens. The federal government's decision to
prosecute prompted an active lobby effort. In addition to the cities
mentioned, more than 400 religious congregations declared themselves sanctuaries, and the list has grown. Sanctuary advocates

have justified their actions based on religious precedent and the general feeling that the United States is acting in violation of the 1980 Refugee Act, which provides that asylum be given to those refugees fleeing political persecution.

American public opinion supported the concerns of sanctuary activists, seriously questioning the Reagan administration's continued support of the Salvadoran government under Napoleon Duarte's leadership. In a May 1984 Harris survey following Duarte's election, only 9% of those surveyed perceived El Salvador as a close ally, 29% viewed the country as friendly, 32% not friendly, 11% as enemy, and 19% were not sure.[53] In contrast, the Reagan administration interpreted the election as legitimizing continued U.S. support for the Duarte administration and its continued alliance with the United States. This assumption did not acknowledge the contention that 25% of the country was still controlled by leftist guerrillas, backed by Cuba and Nicaragua, who did not participate in the electoral process.

Changing U.S. Foreign Policy:
A Question of Local Geography?

These issues and local actions taken on them have been reviewed, and several interesting similarities can be observed. For the most part, these political issues appeared on local agendas primarily because of the actions of national interest groups. These groups, frustrated with their limited influence at the national level and inability to bring about policy revisions, sought alternate paths of persuasion. According to Will Swaim, former associate director of the Center for Innovative Diplomacy, the rationale for targeting cities can be defined as follows:

1. Sheer numbers—there are more than 500,000 local elected officials across the United States.
2. Accessibility.
3. The arms race takes an inordinate amount of money away from possible local revenues; for example, it causes the death of revenue sharing.

4. City officials have a legal and moral obligation to pursue peaceful, nonviolent conflict resolution and can project this approach.
5. Elected officials are democratically elected, giving them a level of legitimacy that translates into greater influence.[54]

The public developed a new consciousness in the 1980s, which was receptive to these overtures as it lost faith in traditional foreign policy leaders. As noted in the previous discussion, public opinion was supportive of the types of policies promoted by interest groups at the local level. Perhaps the most telling in this regard is the extent to which the public approved or disapproved of the Reagan administration's handling of foreign policy. The Gallup Poll found the approval rate to be 37% in 1987 compared with 57% in 1986.[55] Gallup believes that the Iran-Contra scandal is the one event most affecting this change.

Cities increasingly became an outlet for the expression of these concerns. Many local leaders believed it was their responsibility to act on international issues. As the former mayor of Los Angeles Tom Bradley noted in his address to the 1985 Congress of the National League of Cities:

> I submit to you that cities have the right, indeed, even the obligation, to be part of the great national debate in these weighty issues. From foreign trade policies to opposing South African apartheid, from immigration policies to the proliferation of nuclear weapons. The right of cities to be heard on these crucial issues derives from two fundamental principles. First, local government is closest to the people. In fact, one of the few ways citizens can register their dissent is through locally elected representatives. . . . [Second,] many of our national policies are felt first—and in the end most profoundly—in America's cities.[56]

Despite this view, it is interesting to note that not all cities have been active on foreign policy issues, while many of the same cities have spoken out on a number of other issues. Large metropolitan areas, including New York, Chicago, and Los Angeles, have acted on two or more of the four issues discussed here. There are also smaller cities (e.g., Brookline, Massachusetts; Santa Cruz, California; and Tucson, Arizona) that have been very active. What unites these cities in their foreign policy bids?

Notes

1. Foresberg, R. (1980). *Call to halt nuclear arms race*. Brookine, MA: Institute for Defense and Disarmament Studies.

2. Shuman, M. H. (1986-1987) Dateline main street: Local foreign policies. *Foreign Policy, 65,* 154-174.

3. Gallup, Jr., G. (1983). *The Gallup poll: Public opinion 1982*. Wilmington, DE: Scholarly Resources.

4. Gallup, Jr., G. (1985). *The Gallup poll: Public opinion 1984*. Wilmington, DE: Scholarly Resources.

5. Hastings, E. H., & Hastings, P. K. (Eds.). (1986). *Index to international public opinion, 1984-1985*. New York: Greenwood Press.

6. Hastings & Hastings (1986).

7. Nuclear Weapons Freeze Campaign. (1985, October). *The Nuclear Weapons Freeze Campaign* (Information sheet). Washington, DC: NWFC.

8. Interview, July 2, 1986. Larry Agran was also a ciy councilman in Irvine, California, and the Populist presidential candidate for 1992. The Local Elected Officials group is the result of a merger between LEO-USA and LEO-SR, both founded in 1983. They later merged with the Center for Innovative Diplomacy.

9. Agran, L. (1984, November 18). Tragic consequences of arms race. *Los Angeles Times,* sec. 4, p. 4. Quoted with permission from the author.

10. New partnership forged in Nevada desert. (1987-1988). *Bulletin of Municipal Foreign Policy, 2,* 14.

11. "New Partnership Forged" (1987-1988, p. 14).

12. Congress calls for nuclear test ban. (1986, April). *Washington Peace Letter, 23,* 1.

13. Telephone interview with Andrew Tonkavitch, coordinator, Westside Los Angeles SANE/Freeze, July 19, 1988.

14. Plans for commemorating test ban treaty are finalized. (1988). *Bulletin of Municipal Foreign Policy, 2,* 24.

15. A look back and ahead at a nuclear test ban. (1988). *Bulletin of Municipal Foreign Policy, 2,* 25.

16. "Plans for Commemorating" (1988, p. 24).

17. Telephone interview, July 19, 1988.

18. Gallup, Jr., G. (1987). *The Gallup poll: Public opinion 1986*. Wilmington, DE: Scholarly Resources. (Quote from p. 108)

19. Gallup (1987).

20. Gallup, G., Jr. (1988). *The Gallup poll: Public opinion 1987*. Wilmington, DE: Scholarly Resources.

21. Gallup (1988).

22. Nuclear Free Zone Registry. (1985). *Paths to empowerment: A nuclear free zone primer* [pamphlet]. Lake Elsinore, CA: Nuclear Free Zone Registry.

23. Hawaii County was actually the first U.S. municipality to declare itself a nuclear free zone in 1981 but it did not receive the press recognition Garrett Park's action generated.

24. Hastings, E. H., & Hastings, P. K. (Eds.). (1990). *Index to international public opinion, 1988-1989*. New York: Greenwood Press.

25. Personal communication, Jeb Brugmann, June 5, 1986.

26. Campaign Against Investment in South Africa. (n.d.). Divest from apartheid: Invest in the U.S.A. [pamphlet]. Washington, DC: Washington Office on Africa.

27. Bateman, S. C., & Pohlmann, K. (1984, June). State investments in South Africa: Trends in divestment legislation. *Backgrounder* [Council of State Governments], pp. 1-12. (Quotes from p. 5)

28. Kempster, N. S. (1987, February 11). Africa policy a failure, adminstration panel says. *Los Angeles Times*, sec. 1, p. 1.

29. Shannon, D. (1987, February 21). U.S. and Britain veto proposal for U.N. economic sanctions on S. Africa. *Los Angeles Times*, sec. 1, p. 9.

30. Gallup, Jr., G. (1986). *The Gallup poll: Public opinion 1985*. Wilmington, DE: Scholarly Resources.

31. Gallup (1986).

32. Gallup (1987).

33. Gallup (1987).

34. Hastings & Hastings (1986).

35. Hastings, E., & Hastings, P. K. (Eds.). (1988). *Index to international public opinion, 1986-1987*. New York: Greenwood Press.

36. Hastings & Hastings (1986).

37. Hastings & Hastings (1988).

38. Hastings & Hastings (1988).

39. Hastings & Hastings (1988).

40. Hastings, E. H., & Hastings, P. K. (Eds.). (1992). *Index to international public opinion, 1990-1991*. New York: Greenwood Press; and Gallup, Jr., G. (1991). *The Gallup poll: Public opinion 1990*. Wilmington, DE: Scholarly Resources.

41. Love, J. (1985). *The U.S. anti-apartheid movement: Local activism in global politics*. New York: Praeger.

42. Jurisdictions passing divestiture measures exceed 110. (1987-1988). *Bulletin of Municipal Foreign Policy, 2*, 45.

43. Shuman (1986-1987).

44. Interview with Homer Page, February 14, 1986.

45. 39 mayors sign anti-Contra initiative. (1988). *Bulletin of Municipal Foreign Policy, 2*, 28.

46. Gallup (1988).

47. Gallup (1986).

48. Gallup (1987).

49. Gallup (1988).

50. Gallup, Jr., G. (1989). *The Gallup poll: Public opinion 1988*. Wilmington, DE: Scholarly Resources.

51. *Refugee legal support service* [pamphlet]. (n.d.). Austin, TX: Refugee Legal Support Service.

52. An interesting comparison of these movements can be found in Villarruel, K. L. (1987). The underground railroad and the sanctuary movement: A comparison of history, litigation, and values. *Southern California Law Review, 60*, 1429-1463.

53. Hastings & Hastings (1986).

54. Swaim, W. (1988, April 30). *Economic security through economic change*. Paper presented at the the the Conference on Mutually Assured Development, Irvine, CA.

55. Gallup (1988).

56. Bradley, T. (1987). Municipal Responsibility in International Affairs. In M. H. Shuman (Ed.), *Building municipal foreign policies: An action handbook* (pp. 4-6). Irvine, CA: Center for Innovative Diplomacy. (Quote from p. 4)

3

Main Street America
Goes International

Changing public opinion and the activities of interest groups have been successful only to the degree to which cities have been responsive. The operatives of municipal foreign policy are the local governments of cities across the United States. What brings these cities together in their foreign policy pursuits? A total of 353 cities have acted on one or more of the targeted issues—comprehensive test ban, nuclear free zone, divestment, and sanctuary. They represent 44 states from coast to coast. At a glance, they may seem to have little in common. A closer look, however, reveals some interesting nuances that support a commonality of interests and experience in the cities that have chosen to become active on international issues.

Commonalities in Local Foreign Policy Actors

To understand better the nature of cities active on international issues, four types of characteristics or possible sources of influence can be identified: location, demographic characteristics, socio-economic measures, and form of government. Specifically, locational observations refer to the geographical location and size of the active cities. Is the responsiveness of certain cities to international issues influenced by their location—West, Midwest, Northeast, South—or their size? Has the decline of the Northeast and subsequent southern development been important to local interest and actions on foreign affairs? Are large urban areas more likely to act internationally than small, rural townships?

Second, demographic characteristics may be critical to local governments' involvement in foreign affairs. Are there certain constituencies that are more likely to be responsive to interest group overtures and forays into the international policy arena? In addition to population size and growth, more particular observations about constituency composition, specifically minority representation, may be useful. The progressive radical movement described in Chapter 1 has tried to be particularly sensitive to minority demands and their feelings of distance from the policy process. Yet, while declaring their affinity and support for minority rights, Clavel notes that in the cities he identified for analysis, the building of coalitions with minorities has been limited.[1] Nevertheless, in regard to specific issues such as divestment, active cities are more likely to have a higher than average percentage of blacks. Similarly, a higher than average percentage of Hispanics may be expected in cities that have acted on the sanctuary issue.

Socioeconomic characteristics tell us something about the relative economic well-being of the citizens of a community. By examining education, income levels, percentage of population above or below the poverty level, and housing, some insight is gained into the local constituencies of active cities. The responsiveness of cities to international issues may be a function of the nature of its constituency. In his famous study of patterns of influence, Merton found a local-cosmopolitan dichotomy in terms of individuals' orientation toward their community and beyond.[2] Although locals tended to be older and more attached to their locale, cosmopolitans were younger, with a broader range of educational experience. The cosmopolitan distinction mirrors the middle-class radical image developed by Kann, which is distinguished by a broader outlook, youth, and advanced educational opportunity. Cities with a larger percentage of their population meeting these characteristics may be more likely to act on international issues.

Finally, the extent to which a city is receptive to international concerns may depend on the power structure in operation and city government itself. The type of local governing structure may be critical to the way in which issues move through the system as they hold back or facilitate the types of inputs that successfully gain the attention of decision makers. Much of the reform movement in local government at the turn of the century centered around the shortcomings of special-interest politics that characterized the traditional mayor-council or boss-machine forms of local government. The reformers pushed for the establishment of the council-manager system to ensure greater representation. The new progressivism has challenged both forms of government, seeking reforms that will enhance public participation at all levels of administration. The question to be examined here is whether mayor-councils or council-manager local governments act more readily on broader policy issues, such as the test ban or divestment. Which form of government is the more active agent of local foreign policy?

To examine these variables, a statistical profile of cities active on one or more of the identified issues was prepared. A list of all cities active on the target issues was compiled from information provided by various national lobby organizations. Lists of these cities, identified by issue, can be found in the appendixes. Observations on demographic and socioeconomic characteristics of the active cities are available using 1980 and 1990 U.S. Bureau of Census data.[3] The following discussion reviews the results of this analysis.

Regional Distinctions of Active Cities

By combining the lists of cities active on each of the four issues and editing for cities acting on more than one issue, an active group of cities can be identified. There are 44 states and the District of Columbia encompassed in this group. A summary of the

Table 3.1   Cities by Geographic Distribution

Issue	West	Midwest	Northeast	South	Total
Test ban	31 (19%)	18 (11%)	105 (66%)	6 (4%)	160
Free zone	46 (29%)	36 (23%)	65 (41%)	12 (7%)	159
Divestment	26 (25%)	24 (23%)	25 (24%)	28 (27%)	103
Sanctuary	14 (50%)	7 (25%)	6 (21%)	1 (4%)	28
Activist	22 (33%)	13 (19%)	25 (37%)	7 (10%)	67
Active total	82 (23%)	66 (19%)	167 (47%)	38 (11%)	353

geographical regions represented on each issue is presented in Table 3.1. A fifth category, activist cities, refers to those cities that have moved on more than one of the targeted issues. A list of these cities and the issues they have acted on can be found in the appendixes along with a geographical breakdown by state for all four issues, the activist cities, and the combined group.

Activism among cities on the international issues examined here appears to be a regional phenomenon. Various regions and specific states are particularly active on the issues generally and in regard to specific issues as well. As seen in Table 3.1, 47% of the 353 cities that make up the total are located in the Northeast. Of that figure, Massachusetts with 50 active cities and New Jersey with 55 constitute 63% of the Northeast total. For all issues with the exception of sanctuary, the Northeast is the most active region. The western region is the second most represented area in the sample with 23% of the active cities. Of that figure, California with 46 active cities accounts for 56% of the western total. The western region is the most active on the sanctuary issue, constituting 50% of the total, possibly due to its border territory and relatively larger Hispanic population, which may be more sensitive to this issue.

For the most part, the South-Sun Belt area is the least active with 11% of the total cities represented. Similar results apply to the activist cities, and on every issue except divestment, where the South is in the lead. In this case, ethnic loyalties may cut across political motivations as black constituencies appeal to local legislators for action on the apartheid issues. The result is a broader geographical dispersion of cities active on divestment with 25%

in the West, 23% in the Midwest, 24% in the Northeast, and a large 27% in the South.

The greater showing for the Northeast and particularly Massachusetts and New Jersey overall is primarily influenced by city actions on the nuclear issues—comprehensive test ban and nuclear free zone. At least 32 cities in Massachusetts have acted on the test ban issue and 44 in New Jersey. On the nuclear free zone issue, 29 Massachusetts cities have been active and 14 New Jersey cities.

California activism is not as skewed by the nuclear issues; however, they do enjoy a greater response than the other issues, as 26 cities have declared themselves to be nuclear free. However, only 17 have acted on the comprehensive test ban compared with 20 cities active on divestment and 10 on sanctuary. It is interesting to note that the numbers for divestment and sanctuary represent the greatest concentration of support for these issues in any one state. California accounts for 19% of those cities active on the divestment issue, and 36% of cities active on sanctuary.

These observations suggest local activism may be not only a regional phenomenon but a product of activist states as well, specifically, Massachusetts, New Jersey, and California. Other states in the double digits include New York with 18 active cities, Wisconsin with 17, Connecticut with 16, Ohio with 13, Rhode Island with 12, and Michigan and Pennsylvania with 10 each (see the appendixes). Although the focus of this study is not on states, it is possible that cities located within these states are more inclined to act on international issues in the tradition of what Duchacek has identified as "me-tooism," wherein local leaders see political opportunity as a result of local activism in other communities and respond in kind.[4] A second reason may result from a more favorable political climate in certain areas that find such actions socially acceptable. California is a good example here.

A third rationale may be supported by the location of these active states and their economic status. The majority of active cities are found in what is increasingly referred to as the Snow Belt, or Rust Belt, the Northeastern corridor traditionally dominated by heavy industry and now in a state of decline.[5] The economic growth areas are found to the South, or Sun Belt and are dominated by service industries. Action on international issues may distract from the more pressing problems experienced in the Rust Belt, while Sun Belt cities are too busy with economic development to be involved.

Big Cities, Small Cities, and Those In-between

With the geographical location of these cities now identified, more specific characteristics and questions about the cities themselves can be examined. Along these lines: How big are the active cities in terms of size and population? Two bases of comparison are developed due to differences in data definitions from one census to the next. The first comes from the 1980 census data for all places with populations of 2,500 or more, including the active cities; these are identified as "1980 All" and the total number is 9,969. The second base of comparison comes from the 1990 census data for places with populations of 10,000 or more combined with place data for six states that are characterized by townships with a population less than 10,000.[6] The total number of combined cases for "1990 All" is 3,965.

As illustrated in Table 3.2 in terms of land area, most of the cities are quite large compared with the 1980 and 1990 cumulative place data. Although the nuclear free zone cities are still quite small (6.8 mi^2 in 1980), the average size of the 1980 active group is 15.2 mi^2, with activist cities having an average of 32.8 mi^2. The divestment cities are the largest, encompassing an average of 34.5 mi^2. This observation suggests larger cities have been more responsive to divestment and supports the argument that this issue has more often been the product of cross-cutting cleavages along racial lines, due to greater black population representation in large urban areas, rather than the other concerns. This point is reinforced by the relatively large black populations in the divestment cities, discussed below.

The growth in land area by issue for 1990 represents not only additional cities that have adopted resolutions supporting divestment and nuclear free zone declarations but city annexation as well.[7] Frequently, to solve inner city problems, cities have expanded their

Table 3.2 Land Area and Population

Variables	Test Ban	Nuclear Free Zone	Divestment	Sanctuary	Activist	Active	All
Land area (mi²)							
1980	15.2	6.8	34.5	22.6	32.8	15.2	5.8
1990	18.9	14.1	46.3	29.8	38.8	21.9	11.4
Population							
1970	41,832	15,574	165,655	85,288	137,707	38,880	5,133
1980	39,711	16,267	159,611	84,748	126,109	39,406	6,597
1990	47,025	36,073	156,813	85,571	133,542	52,277	19,048
Population change (%)							
1970-1980	-5.0	+4.3	-3.6	-0.6	-8.4	+1.3	+22.1
1980-1990	+18.0	+127.0	-1.7	+1.0	+5.8	+33.0	NA
Black population (%)							
1980	2.6	2.1	22.5	4.2	22.6	3.4	1.1
1990	4.7	3.7	19.9	4.1	18.6	7.7	2.9
Hispanic population (%)							
1980	3.2	3.0	3.1	4.7	8.0	3.0	1.2
1990	6.3	3.7	4.8	7.7	8.0	5.1	2.3

NA = not applicable.

borders to enhance their tax bases. This is particularly true of the more urban divestment and activist cities.

In terms of population, the active cities are also quite large. As noted in Table 3.2, the average 1980 median population value for the national data set is 6,597. In contrast, the average value for the active group is almost six times that total with a population of 39,406. The nuclear free zone cities are less than half the size of the active group, compared with the other extreme, divestment cities, which are four times larger. Activist cities also enjoyed a fairly large average population; it was 126,109 in 1980. Sanctuary is not far behind with 84,748, whereas test ban cities are closest to the overall national value. The larger population figures, especially for divestment and the activist cities, reinforce greater urban support for local foreign policy. Figures for 1990 uphold these observations.

Urban areas have been the hardest hit in terms of population declines in recent years. The relative changes in population from 1970 to 1980 and 1980 to 1990 support an urban concentration for two of the issues and the activist cities. Divestment cities on the average showed a 3.6% loss in their populations from 1970 to 1980, which continued from 1980 to 1990 with a decline of approximately 2%. The loss was even greater for test ban cities from 1970 to 1980 with a decline of 5%; however, they were able to turn this trend around from 1980 to 1990 with a significant growth rate of 18%. Activist cities generally lost out in the 1970s with a decline of 8.4%, but they were also able to regain some ground in the 1980s with an increase of 5.8%.

Nuclear free zone cities were big winners in terms of population in the 1980s. While experiencing modest growth in the 1970s (4.3%), they more than doubled in size in the 1980s, with 127% growth. Sanctuary cities stayed fairly stable, going from a loss in population of 0.6% from 1970 to 1980 to an increase of 1% from 1980 to 1990. The active group generally experienced very little growth in the 1970s, with only 1.3%, but increased significantly in the 1980s with a net gain 33% of their 1980 population.

Furthermore, minority representation defined as the percentage of the population made up of blacks and Hispanics was higher for all issue cities than the national data set in both 1980 and 1990.

As can be seen in Table 3.2, the black appeal of the divestment issue is borne out with a substantial average of 22.5% of the population identified as black compared with 3.4% for the active group and only 1.1% for the total data set in 1980 and 19.9% compared with 7.7% for the active group and 2.9% overall for 1990. Similarly, Hispanics are more highly represented on the sanctuary issue with 4.7% compared with 3% for the active cities and only 1.2% for the total in 1980 and 7.7% compared with 5.1% for the sample and 2.3% for the total in 1990.

Higher minority figures also characterize the activist cities. This is due to the high representation both divestment and sanctuary enjoy in the activist sample; 50 of the 103 divestment cities (49%) and 23 of the 28 sanctuary cities (82%) are considered activist cities, i.e., having acted on more than one of the targeted issues. There does not seem to be much correlation between the two issues, however, because there are only 22 cities (33%) that have acted on both issues in the activist group. A somewhat stronger correlation can be drawn out between the test ban and nuclear free zone issues (27 cases in common; 40%) but even more so for test ban and divestment issues (37 cases in common; 55%). It might be concluded that success on one issue gives momentum to supporters for another, and although the nuclear issues intuitively might be grouped together (as could the minority rights issues), the relationship between divestment and the comprehensive test ban on face value is not clear.

Constituency-Driven Local Foreign Policy

If local actions on foreign policy are a product of the middle-class radicalism that Kann, Clavel, and others have identified as emerging in American cities today, then figures for higher education may be greater for cities active on international issues. On all issues, the figures for people 25 or more years old who at least graduated high school vary from 1980 to 1990 as seen in Table 3.3. In 1980, all the issue groups were higher than the national data set, with the exception of divestment. Nuclear free zone cities had the most educated population, followed closely by sanctuary cities and the test ban cities; the activist cities came in fourth.

In contrast, data for 1990 show nuclear free zone cities and the activist cities dipping below the total data set. The active group as a whole is only slightly higher (0.2%) than the national group, which is not significant. The divestment cities show the only consistent pattern from 1980 to 1990, as they continued to deviate from the group with the percentage of the population having a high school or better education 3% below the national group in 1980, which increased to 6% below in 1990. Figures for people 25 or more years old without a high school diploma also support these trends, as all the issue groups are below the national data percentage, with the exception of the divestment and activist cities for both 1980 and 1990.

A second measurement of constituency well-being is the percentage of the population above or below the poverty level. If local activism is a product of changing urban environments and their responsiveness to distanced populations, then it might be expected that those cities that have acted on international issues would have more people below the poverty level and less persons above the national level. Such is the case as illustrated in Table 3.4 for both 1980 and 1990 with a minor exception. Nuclear free zones cities in the 1980s were slightly below the national figure, i.e., they had fewer people below the poverty level than the national average. The extremes below the poverty level are again the divestment and activist cities.

Similar results are found for the percentage of population above the poverty level (Table 3.4). Although the median value for this observation seems high at 87% in 1980 and 88% in 1990, none of the issue groups meet or exceed that figure. Comprehensive test ban cities come closest in 1980 with 86% of their population above the poverty level, and sanctuary cities come the closest in 1990 with 85%. The activist group is the lowest in 1980 at 74%, while divestment cities are the lowest in 1990 with 76%. These observations do not generally support the middle-class radical profile; however, it is possible to suggest that the middle-class radicals are a minority in the cities in which they are most active.

Table 3.3 Education Level for People 25 or More Years Old

Education Level	Test Ban	Nuclear Free Zone	Divestment	Sanctuary	Activist	Active	All
High school or more (%)							
1980	45	49	37	47	44	42	40
1990	53	49	44	55	47	51	50
Grade 11 or less (%)							
1980	16	11	19	12	22	15	18
1990	12	7	15	12	16	11	13

Table 3.4 Population Relative to Poverty Level

Poverty Level	Test Ban	Nuclear Free Zone	Divestment	Sanctuary	Activist	Active	All
Below the poverty level (%)							
1980	9.0	8.0	15.0	13.0	19.0	11.0	8.3
1990	9.0	11.0	18.0	16.0	21.0	12.0	7.7
Above the poverty level (%)							
1980	86.0	81.0	81.5	80.0	74.0	83.0	87.0
1990	82.0	78.0	76.0	85.0	78.0	86.5	88.0

Another variable that reveals something about the relative economic status of a community is income. Two figures can be examined for the issue cities: per capita income and median household income. As can be seen in Table 3.5, the national average per capita income for 1980 is $6,952. All of the issue groups, the active group, and activist cities exceed this figure with the exception of divestment at $6,906. The higher figures are not, however, radically different; sanctuary cities have the greatest per capita income at $7,954, which is 14% higher than the national average per capita figure. These trends are reinforced by the 1990 data; divestment cities are again the exception and are joined by the activist cities for this time period.

These observations do not hold up, however, for median household income. Here the averages for the national data sets in both 1980 and 1990 are higher than all of the other issues, the activist cities, and the active group. The test ban and nuclear free zone cities are the closest to the national figure, with divestment the farthest from the median value in both time periods.

A final constituency characteristic that may be considered is housing, particularly renter or owner occupancy (Table 3.6). Many of those who fall into the progressive profile are renters. It is significant that all of the issue groups are exceedingly high in this area. While the national median value represents 25% of the population in renter-occupied housing in 1980, the activist group has by far the greatest with 60%. Sanctuary runs a close second, and divestment is not far behind. Test ban cities are almost even with the active group as a whole at about 47%—almost double the national value—and nuclear free zone cities have an average of 42% renter-occupied housing. Similarly, in 1990, the overall national percentage is also significantly exceeded by all of the issue groups. Activist cities continue to show the greatest deviance in terms of renter-occupied housing (62%) compared with the national average of 33%; the sanctuary cities are at 57% and test ban and divestment cities are not far behind (53%).

In terms of the value of housing, all of the issue, activist, and active cities exceeded the national value in 1980. Divestment cities had the lowest average housing value in 1980, which carried over into 1990. The divestment cities were the only group below the

Table 3.5 Income (in dollars)

Income	Test Ban	Nuclear Free Zone	Divestment	Sanctuary	Activist	Active	All
Per capita							
1980	7,483	7,259	6,906	7,954	7,176	7,367	6,952
1990	15,862	15,161	13,695	15,269	14,564	14,710	14,681
Median household							
1980	16,266	16,378	14,226	15,339	14,604	15,993	17,150
1990	33,140	31,527	26,599	29,044	27,175	29,578	33,750

Table 3.6 Housing

Housing	Test Ban	Nuclear Free Zone	Divestment	Sanctuary	Activist	Active	All
Units							
1980	14,545	6,620	61,315	35,508	52,041	14,680	2,507
1990	17,118	14,676	67,092	36,270	57,332	21,988	7,586
Renter occupied (%)							
1980	47.5	42.0	49.0	54.0	60.0	47.0	25.0
1990	53.0	40.0	53.0	57.0	62.0	45.0	33.0
Value ($)							
1980	56,550	59,850	48,000	65,950	56,800	54,800	43,600
1990	145,000	139,900	78,750	115,800	114,650	116,500	91,400

total data set for that time period, while test ban and nuclear free zone cities made great gains. The generally higher cost of housing suggests an urban concentration for the active cities as most urban areas have faced housing value inflation over the last few years.

The figures for income and housing take on more meaning when compared with one another. Specifically, to what extent has the buying power of households increased or decreased relative to housing? Table 3.7 illustrates the ratio of income to housing value expressed as a percentage. The result is that from 1980 to 1990, despite significant increases in income, the real buying power of that income relative to housing actually decreased generally with the exception of divestment and sanctuary cities.

These observations take on greater meaning when compared with a sample of nonactive cities for both 1980 and 1990. As illustrated in Table 3.8, the statements made up to this point are reinforced by the nonactive data. Active cities are significantly larger in size and population with greater minority representation than nonactive cities. They have a greater percentage of their population below the poverty level and are economically less well off in terms of median household income. They consist of almost double the number of renters and are faced with extremely high housing costs.

The Structure
of Local Governments

Beyond demographic and socioeconomic characteristics is the city government itself. The percentages for the different types of local government structures for all of the issue groups, the activist cities, and the active group are presented in Table 3.9. Five governmental types are represented: mayor-council, council-manager, town meeting, representative town meeting, and commission.[8] The mayor-council form of government is characterized by an elected chief executive officer, the mayor, with variations in the scope of policy-making authority, while the chief administrative officer in the council-manager form of government is a manager appointed by

Table 3.7 Ratio of Median Household Income to Housing Value (%)

Year	Test Ban	Nuclear Free Zone	Divestment	Sanctuary	Activist	Active	All
1980	28.7	27.3	29.6	23.3	25.7	29.1	39.3
1990	22.8	22.5	33.7	25.0	23.7	25.3	36.9

Table 3.8   Comparison of Nonactive, Active, and Activist Cities

Characteristic	Nonactive	Active	Activist
Land Area (mi^2)			
1980	5.3	15.2	32.8
1990	11.4	21.9	38.8
Population			
1970	5,399	38,830	137,707
1980	6,303	39,406	126,109
1990	18,400	52,277	133,542
Population change (%)			
1970-1980	+14.0	+1.3	−8.4
1980-1990	NA	+32.6	+5.8
Black population (%)			
1980	1.2	3.4	22.6
1990	2.7	7.7	18.6
Hispanic population (%)			
1980	1.2	3.0	8.0
1990	2.3	5.1	8.0
Education level (people 25 or more years old)			
High school or more (%)			
1980	44.2	42.0	44.3
1990	50.7	50.7	47.4
Grade 11 or less (%)			
1980	18.9	15.1	22.0
1990	12.9	11.4	16.3
Poverty level (%)			
Below			
1980	8.0	11.0	19.1
1990	7.6	12.1	20.8
Above			
1980	90.0	82.9	74.0
1990	87.6	86.5	78.1
Per capita income ($)			
1980	6,974	7,367	7,176
1990	14,681	14,710	14,564
Median household income ($)			
1980	17,433	15,993	14,604
1990	34,060	29,578	27,175
Housing			
Units			
1980	2,446	14,680	52,041
1990	7,305	21,988	57,332

(Continued)

Table 3.8   Continued

Characteristic	Nonactive	Active	Activist
Renter occupied (%)			
1980	25.0	47.0	60.0
1990	29.8	44.6	62.0
Value ($)			
1980	44,900	54,800	56,800
1990	90,700	116,500	114,650
Ratio median household			
income to housing value (%)			
1980	38.8	29.1	25.7
1990	37.5	25.3	23.7

NA = not applicable.

and responsible to an elected council. The manager has little, if any, policy-making authority.

In contrast, all voters directly participate in the town meeting to establish policy, selecting a few citizens to carry out the decisions made by the group. The representative town meeting is quite similar; however, although all citizens may participate in the meetings, only a selected number may vote. Finally, the commission form of government consists of an elected commission that performs both executive and legislative tasks.

Nationally, the mayor-council form of government is the most popular, followed by the council-manager, commission, town meeting, and representative town meeting.[9] Interestingly, however, is the relationship of population to form of government. Smaller cities with populations of 5,000 or more are dominated by the mayor-council governments but are strongly represented in the commission, town meeting, and representative town meeting structures as well. This trend reverses with cities of 10,000 or more to 100,000 or more: Council-manager systems dominate these cities. In the largest cities—those with populations of 250,000 or more to 1,000,000 or more—the mayor-council system is by far the dominant form of government.

Of the active cities for which data were available (264 cases or 75%), the mayor-council form of government (43%) only slightly exceeds the council-manager form of government (42%).[10] The

Table 3.9 Percentage of Different Forms of Local Governments

Form	Test Ban	Nuclear Free Zone	Divestment	Sanctuary	Activist	Active
Mayor-council	52.0	35.5	44.0	50.0	54.0	43.0
Council-manager	29.0	45.5	51.0	46.0	40.0	42.0
Town meeting	7.0	14.0	1.0	4.0	2.0	7.0
Representative town meeting	3.0	3.0	1.0	0.0	4.0	2.0
Commission	8.0	1.0	3.0	0.0	0.0	5.0

SOURCE: Data from International City Management Association (1985, 1986, 1988, 1990).

test ban, sanctuary, and activist cities all have a larger proportion of the mayor-council form of government than the active group, with the test ban cities the greatest at 66%.

The second most favored government structure is the council-manager form, the objective of the urban reform movement in the early 1900s. Divestment cities are the leader here with an average of 51%, followed closely by sanctuary cities with 46% and nuclear free zones with 45.5%. The divestment group is dominated by California cities, which have overwhelmingly adopted the council-manager form of government. Only the large urban areas, such as Los Angeles and San Francisco, have maintained a mayor-council form of government, supporting the national trends identified in relation to population. Nuclear free zone cities are unique in that they have the highest percentage of town meeting governments with 14%. This is a reflection of the location of many of these cities in the Northeast, particularly Massachusetts. The activist cities have 40% council-manager governments and test ban cities have 29%. The total for the active group is 42%.

What does the preponderance of mayor-council governments for the activist cities indicate about local activism on international issues? As noted in Chapter 1, urban scholars have observed that unreformed city governments, distinguished by the mayor-council system, partisan elections, and ward constituencies, are more likely to be responsive to groups and various interests in the population than are reformed governments, distinguished by a manager system, at-large constituencies, and nonpartisan elections.[11] Certainly some of the more prominent international political issues that cities have concerned themselves with have been the product of mayoral characteristics and concerns. New York City emerges as one of the most active cities on these issues, having acted on all four. Both former mayor Ed Koch and former mayor David Dinkins have personally been involved in international affairs since taking office. A similar argument can be made for former mayor Tom Bradley of Los Angeles and former mayors Andrew Young and Maynard Jackson of Atlanta, to name only a few.

In contrast, the city of Boulder, Colorado, has also acted on all four issues and is governed by a council-manager form of government. According to David Grimm, public liaison for the city,

Boulder has a very participatory governmental system that has pursued a slow-growth strategy.[12] Here the nature of the constituents needs to be more closely examined as the reputation of the city and attraction of a major university located in the area have resulted in an active lobby effort. Grimm suggests that many of the local activists who have come to Boulder were part of more formal activist groups in the past but are no longer affiliated with them. They have, however, taken the skills developed in these movements to city hall to bring about a more representative local government.

Often, activists have been drawn to cities based on the opportunities they find there. One particularly attractive draw for many is the presence of a college or university in the area. A cursory assessment of whether there was a university base connection with the active cities defined for the 1980 data set was made.[13] Using various sources, it was found that 53% of the active cities for which information was available had some type of college or university located within or nearby. Of the activist cities, 90% had either a college or university, and in many cases, they had several educational facilities of higher learning. To give this observation perspective, a random sample of nonactive cities was generated from the national data set. Only 14% of this sample had colleges or universities within them.

Profiles of Local
Foreign Policy Actors

Given these observations, what type of profile emerges for active cities on the four issues identified here and how does it compare with current urban perspectives, particularly middle-class radicalism and the new progressive movement? Does the "human scale community" extend beyond the community to the global community at large? A major objective of the new progressive movement is to make city hall more in tune with the people by encouraging participatory democracy. Much of the local activism on international issues has also heralded this cause. In addition, a frequent justification offered by the various national lobby organizations active on these issues cite personal rights as a motivation for local activism.[14]

A conflict emerges, however, in that an overriding objective of the new progressivism has been local change. How does this fit with foreign policy activism? In many instances, international issues may represent an easier goal than changing local government practices. It may be simpler to get local officials to act on something outside the community than to bring about change in the local environment as the immediate effects are less discernible. In addition, the symbolic effect of this action may give support to activist community organizations and strengthen them.

On closer examination, the characterization of cities active on international issues that develops is similar to the profile of cities that have been responsive to progressive overtures. All of the cities identified by Kann and Clavel are included in the list of active cities. In terms of a profile, much of the new progressive movement has emerged in northeastern cities greatly affected by the changing international economy or the western cities seeking protection from the inevitable negative consequences of rapid growth. They are predominantly urban areas with strong minority representation. Disparities in education, income levels, and housing value are typical. A high percentage of housing renters as opposed to owners is also common. The distinction in terms of form of government is less clear; however, the radical movement has infiltrated all types of governing structures. The active cities on foreign policy issues mirror many of these same characteristics. A breakdown by issue illustrates these similarities.

The comprehensive test ban movement has had the widest appeal due to the methods employed by local and national freeze organizations, which capitalized on existing structures established in the late 1970s and early 1980s to lobby for a nuclear freeze; yet, the test ban cities are more exclusive generally than the other issue city groups. They are smaller in size and population, with the exception of the nuclear free zone cities. They were also hardest hit in terms of population decline in the 1970s, although this trend has changed in the 1980s, and population growth is coming back. Minority representation is limited.

Test ban cities have improved their level of educational attainment within their populations in the last 10 years. While high school education and beyond was important to this group in the 1980 data, it still ranked behind both the nuclear free zone and sanctuary groups. By 1990, these cities were exceeded only by sanctuary cities and by a very small (2%) margin.

The populations of these cities are generally better off than the other issue cities. They have consistently had the fewest people below the poverty level in both 1980 and 1990 compared with the other issue cities. Conversely, they have the greatest percentage of the population above the poverty level, with the exception of sanctuary cities in 1990. They are generally wealthier than the other issue cities, exceeded only by the sanctuary cities in per capita income in 1980 and nuclear free zone cities in median household income in 1990. Housing figures reinforce this profile; there are fewer renters in test ban cities. Nevertheless, the growth in the cost of housing, despite significant income growth, has resulted in a loss of home purchasing power for constituents in these cities. They are also significantly different in form of government, having the highest percentage of mayor-council governing structures second only to the activist group by 1%. They also have the highest percentage of commission governments.

The nuclear free zone effort has been more specialized, characterized by smaller cities in size and population.[15] These cities, however, have experienced a net growth in terms of population from 1970 to 1980, with an average increase of 4.4%, and tremendous growth from 1980 to 1990, with an increase of 127%. They are the highest of the issues sets in education—an average of 49% of the population of these cities have a high school education or better—exceeded only by the test ban cities in 1990. They are third in per capita income and yet were first in median household income in 1980 and a close second to test ban cities in 1990. The percentage of the population above the poverty level in these cities is not as significant in 1990, with a rank of third compared with the other issues, exceeded only by divestment cities. They still fared better in population below the poverty level in 1990, with test ban cities the only group to have a smaller percentage. Although they are dominated by the council-manager form of government, they have the largest number of town meeting governmental structures. Finally, they are the weakest in terms of minority representation of the four issue groups.

In contrast, divestment actions have been a function of minorities, especially the black population. Divestment cities are very large urban areas with large, less-educated populations; a greater percentage of the population is below the poverty level, and these cities have lower incomes and housing values.

The form of government in divestment cities as a distinguishing feature—51% are mayor-council and 44% are council-manager—supports the thesis that cities with mayoral forms of government are more likely to act in response to specialized constituencies. Furthermore, the number of elected black officials that are a part of those governments is critical. Of 77 divestment cities examined from the 1980 data set, 58 (75%) have at least one and, in most cases, two or more elected black officials.[16] In the sample of all cities examined in 1980 (290), only 94 (32%) had elected black officials.

Sanctuary cities are also urban areas but are concentrated in the West and have the largest Hispanic populations due to their location. Many refugees seeking asylum have come to the western region, particularly the border states, because of the large numbers of refugees already living there and the cultural affinity they share with other Spanish-speaking groups. The sanctuary cities are second only to the divestment cities in size and population. Population growth in the 10-year period from 1970 to 1980 was minimal and increased only slightly from 1980 to 1990. While sanctuary cities were second to the nuclear free zone cities in the percentage of people with a high school education or better in 1980, they were highest in this area in 1990. In terms of per capita income, sanctuary cities were the highest in this area in 1980 and were exceeded only by the test ban cities in 1990. They are also dominated by the mayor-council form of government.

Sanctuary cities had primarily renter-based housing, with the highest figures for both 1980 and 1990 compared with the other issues. The value of housing reinforced this trend in 1980, as the highest value, but ranked third in 1990. The result was a net increase in the home purchasing power, shown in the ratio of median household income to housing value in 1990.

There are 67 cities that have acted on more than one of the target issues, called activist cities. They are perhaps the most representative of many of the trends observed in the data as a whole and the closest to the new progressive city model. Generally, the activist cities are large urban areas with large populations. They are located predominantly in the Northeast (37%), with the second most represented area, the West, at 33%. They have a significant minority population, larger than any of the other issue groups, with the exception of blacks in the divestment cities. The educational attainment of the population within these cities is the weakest compared with the other issue groups; the percentage of those with less than high school education is quite high (22% in 1980 and 16% in 1990).

Economically, the activist cities are also depressed, with the highest figures for population below the poverty level. They do not fare much better in terms of income; they are second only to divestment cities as the lowest in per capita and median household income. Although the housing value is not as high as some of the other issue groups, the ability to buy housing is limited by income and has actually decreased since 1980. As a result, these cities have a very high percentage of renter-occupied housing (62%). To complete the comparison, in terms of governmental form, they are predominantly governed by a mayor-council government (54%).

These profiles reinforce a commonality among the active cities, generally, and the issues, specifically. They also lend support to the new progressive city thesis as they exhibit many of the characteristics of cities most likely to act in new and aggressive ways. In each group, certain factors are more likely to be influential than others, such as form of government or percentage of minority population. These observations support the postulates made at the outset of what might be expected in each of the issue groups and for the active cities as a whole.

Notes

1. Clavel, P. (1986). *The progressive city: Planning and participation, 1969-1984*. New Brunswick, NJ: Rutgers University Press. A similar argument is developed by Browning, R. P., Rogers Marshall, D., & Rabb, D. H. (1984). *Protest is not enough: The struggle of blacks and Hispanics for equality in urban politics*. Berkeley: University of California Press.

2. Merton, R. K. (1968). *Social theory and social structure*. New York: Free Press.

3. Data were gathered using machine-readable versions of 1980 and 1990 U.S. Bureau of Census data. Summaries of the 1980 data can be found in U.S. Bureau of the Census. (1983). *County and city data book, 1983*. Washington, DC: U.S. Government Printing Office. The majority of 1990 data is still only available in machine-readable form at this time. Guides to these data can be found in U.S. Bureau of the Census. (1991). *Census of population and housing, 1990. Summary tape files 1 & 3: Technical documentation*. Washington, DC: U.S. Bureau of the Census.

4. Duchacek, I. D. (1986). *The territorial dimension of politics: Within, among, and across nations*. Boulder: Westview.

5. A very good discussion of these distinctions can be found in Sawers, L., & Tabb, W. K. (Eds.). (1984). *Sunbelt/Snowbelt: Urban development and regional restructuring*. New York: Oxford University Press.

6. The six additional states included with data for cities with populations under 10,000 were Connecticut, Maine, Massachusetts, New Hampshire, Rhode Island, and Vermont.

7. The number of nuclear free zone and divestment cities increased from the data sets used for 1980 and 1990 observations. The additional cities are indicated in the lists of cities by issues in the appendixes. Despite the increases, however, there was less than a 25% discrepancy in the number of cities for which data were available.

8. International City Management Association. (1990). *The municipal year book 1990*. Washington, DC: International City Management Association.

9. International City Management Association (1990).

10. International City Management Association (1990) includes only cities with populations of at least 2,500 in its report on forms of government.

11. Lineberry, R. L., & Sharkansky, I. (1978). *Urban politics and public policy* (3rd ed.). New York: Harper & Row.

12. Interview with David Grimm, February 14, 1986.

13. These data were gathered from the U.S. Post Office's zip code directory and *The World Almanac and Book of Facts*. (1985). New York: Newspaper Enterprise Association. The accuracy of these data leaves some unresolved questions. The zip code listing was the best source available in a workable format for gathering information but was not always complete, hence other sources, including personal knowledge, were used to supplement the data when possible.

14. The Nuclear Weapoons Freeze Campaign, Nuclear Free Zone Registry, and Campaign Against Investment in South Africa have all issued statements to this effect in their strategies for mobilizing local action.

15. The large percentage of missing data for nuclear free zones reinforces the smallness of these cities; there are no data available on them.

16. These observations were compiled from information provided in the Joint Center for Political Studies. (1986). *Black elected officials: A national roster, 1986.* New York: Bowker.

4

The Truth or Consequences
of Local Activism

Local activism has not taken place in a vacuum. Both opposition and support have emerged at all levels of analysis. Although we now know something about the origins and motivations for city actions, the question of consequences remains, not only in terms of the four issues targeted for investigation and the cities that have acted on them but in a broader context in regard to state actions, national responses, and international perceptions. The extent to which these actions have elicited responses beyond the local level is an indication of their relative importance to the foreign policy process.

To assess the consequences of local activism on international issues, it is necessary first to classify that behavior. As a point of departure, political activities have been distinguished for examination, distinct from cultural, diplomatic, and economic actions. When evaluating the effect of these actions, the intent must also be identified. Two sets of categories that relate to the issues examined here are put forth by Michael Shuman, director of the Institute for Policy Studies and former president of the Center for

Innovative Diplomacy (CID), and Peter Spiro, former special assistant to Abraham Sofaer, legal adviser at the U.S. State Department.[1]

Shuman distinguishes three types of municipal foreign policy: consciousness-raising, unilateral actions, and bilateral measures. Consciousness-raising measures are those policies that involve the "collection, analysis and distribution" of information.[2] They include educational activities, research, and lobbying efforts. Unilateral actions involve local exercise of traditional powers, such as policing, zoning and planning, investing and contracting, and litigation. The issues examined here—comprehensive test ban, nuclear free zones, divestment, and sanctuary—would fall under this distinction from Shuman's point of view because they use traditional structures for far-reaching policy goals. The final category, bilateral measures, refers to agreements made by cities with other cities or countries abroad for border coordination, trade, or cultural exchange. Frequently, these activities have taken on a political function as well, such as the unofficial expansion of sister city programs with the former Soviet Union, Nicaragua, and, most recently, Cuba.

Spiro also distinguishes three types of local foreign policy but from a somewhat different perspective. Spiro is concerned with the acceptability of some local behaviors; hence he develops his typology in terms of the potential consequences of these actions. His first category includes those actions that he believes are simply too insignificant to pose a serious challenge to federal authority: *de minimis*. These would include nonbinding resolutions, statements by local leaders, educational programs, and other consciousness-raising activities.[3] The comprehensive test ban movement would fit here. His second category are those types of foreign policy he believes should be local: trade and transborder cooperation. To Spiro, these activities, for the most part, "pose no danger to the effective maintenance of federal foreign policy."[4] His final category comprises those policies that cross the line of acceptability: foreign policy and defense-related measures. This "local interference" in foreign policy from Spiro's perspective, which would include the remaining issues examined here (nuclear free zones, divestment, and sanctuary), poses serious challenges and potential danger to the federal decision-making process in these areas.

These typologies reflect their author's concerns. Shuman has long been a leading advocate of municipal foreign policy and takes a favorable orientation in developing his categories. In contrast, although Spiro does not claim to be representing the State Department in his writing, he is a very convincing spokesman for those opposing local foreign policy and has used the federal government's responses as the basis for his distinctions. There are similarities in their typologies, however, that can be used to evaluate the consequences of local activism and encompass both of these authors' views.

Two concepts can be employed in this regard: expressive versus instrumental behaviors.[5] There is no doubt that those who lobby for local actions on international issues believe they are acting instrumentally; that is, their actions are undertaken for a specific purpose and will bring about a measurable effect. Such is not always the case; in fact, the actions are often more expressive in their effect. Expressive actions primarily serve an awareness-generating function that brings a given issue into the public light or possibly acts as an avenue for the expression of a public interest that otherwise might not get exposure. Both Shuman's and Spiro's first categories—consciousness-raising and *de minimis*—would fit here. Often these actions are called *feel-good responses* because they make their constituents feel good but bring about little change. This distinction is made most frequently by those opposing local foreign policy activism. Instrumental actions, while also making an expressive statement, enjoy a tangible return or specific result that is defined by the action itself. Both Shuman's and Spiro's other categories can be collapsed into this distinction. Although the authors differ on the positive or negative consequences these actions enjoy, they do have an instrumental function as illustrated below.

The four political issues investigated in this study all have an expressive nature due to the departures from U.S. policy that they represent. With the exception of the comprehensive test ban movement, all the issues also have an instrumental component as well. An argument could be made that the comprehensive test ban is also instrumental in that it represents an organized effort that seeks to stop nuclear testing, the consequences of which will benefit all from at least an environmental level, not to mention the global preoccupation with a halt to the arms race. It does not, however, have the immediate and direct payoff that the other issues enjoy vis-à-vis local entities.

In contast, the nuclear free zone declarations not only seek to send a message regarding the continued buildup of nuclear weapons but also have some very real consequences for defense-related industries located in or nearby the NFZ areas. Divestment sends a message of intolerance for the apartheid regime of South Africa as well as alters the financial portfolio of cities, particularly long-term investment holdings. Finally, sanctuary not only condemns the current political atmosphere in particular Central American countries and U.S. tolerance for their regimes but encourages local violation of certain immigration laws promulgated at the federal level.

With these distinctions in mind, it is possible to examine the consequences that local activism and the response specific ac-tions have received at the private, public, national, and interna-tional levels. Up to this point, a fairly positive orientation toward local activism has been taken, but such actions are not without their detractors. This chapter explores some of the opposition to foreign policy initiatives at the local, state, and national levels as well as the relative successes of these movements.

Sources of Opposition to Local Activism

Local involvement in the international arena has met with op-position at all levels of government and from the private sector as well. At the city level, not all local officials and constituencies have been supportive of the growing international involvement of their local officials. Frequently, local officials themselves have spoken out against the expanding international preoccupation of their city councils.

Former Los Angeles city councilman Richard Alatorre makes a very convincing argument in this regard.[6] The first Latino to serve on the L.A. council since 1962, Alatorre was an active member of the California State assembly before being elected to the city council. He now serves as the chairman of the board in charge of the Los Angeles Metropolitan Transit Authority. Alatorre argues local foreign policy is "intellectual dishonesty" because of its limited effects. He suggests that while such actions may make some people feel good (expressive responses), they are "deceitful" to those who thought it would bring about change (instrumental effects): "Until Congress responds, for cities to do anything is beautiful but not real. I like to deal in the real arena. I don't like to use people."

Alatorre believes local foreign policy is dishonest to his constituents, and he wants to do something in the area in which people can bring about change—not just make political statements. For example, in regard to the sanctuary movement, a critical issue in L.A. politics, Alatorre felt it would not bring relief without federal support for more far-reaching changes in relation to the refugees' countries of origin. He was not, however, assessing the potential impact expressive actions may have in changing public consciousness overall on a given issue.

The case of sanctuary in Los Angeles offers a good example of the way in which city officials can become divided over international issues. Initially passing a resolution that declared the city a sanctuary for refugees from El Salvador and Guatemala by a narrow margin (eight to six) in November 1985, the city council later reversed its position in February 1986 in response to strong opposition.[7] Opposed to the resolution, Councilman Ernani Bernardi, with the support and encouragement of Immigration and Naturalization Services (INS) western regional commissioner Harold Ezell, who was instrumental to the opposition, began a petition drive to place the issue on the ballot for the November 1986 elections, calling on the public to approve or reject the resolution. To head off this initiative Councilman Michael Woo, recent Los Angeles mayoral candidate and author of the resolution, sought a compromise that removed the controversial sanctuary designation and in its place put forth a largely symbolic resolution.

The new resolution was unanimously adopted, reaffirming city policy that prevented municipal workers from considering immigration status in the provision of services and urged passage of pending federal legislation to prevent the deportation of Salvadoran refugees until civil strife in that country had abated.[8] Another provision of the resolution called for the establishment of a task force to review the effect of undocumented workers on the city and help develop a local immigration policy. It was opposed by Councilman Alatorre on the grounds that it would "further inflame" the immigration issue.[9] The final result was a watered-down, non-binding resolution that lost the sanctuary designation but retained the intent of the movement.

Other city councils have taken direct action to limit local debate on international issues. The city of San Buenaventura (Ventura), California, went so far as to pass a resolution that declared both national and international policies and actions outside the purview of the city council.[10] Passed in May 1971, the resolution was a response to growing opposition to the Vietnam War and public clamoring for action at all levels of government.

Citing a lack of authority "to make decisions in these matters" and the inability "to change national or international goals," the resolution suggested those seeking change on such policies direct their attention to the representatives elected for this purpose. The resolution concluded as follows:

> Now, therefore, be it resolved, by the City Council of the City of San Buenaventura that they will continue to devote their time and efforts to considering and resolving only those matters of local concern of which they have elected responsibility; and further the City Council will use whatever means available to dissuade those groups or individuals who request their assistance on matters of national or international concern.

The measure passed the council handily by a vote of six to one.

Many constituents have questioned the personal involvement of their city officials in international affairs, concerned that they are ignoring local problems. Former mayor of Los Angeles Tom Bradley received a great deal of criticism for his frequent travels abroad, with more trips than any mayor in the nation's 10 most populous cities.[11] Although Bradley officials justified his trips as important to the international image of Los Angeles and foreign trade activities, the public has not always seen the benefits. This dissatisfaction was so great that the 1993 mayoral race that marked Bradley's retirement and the end of his 20 years of service found him to be noticeably absent from the campaign. The result was this headline in the *Los Angeles Times:* "Send Out a Search Party—Our Mayor Is Missing."[12] Nor is Bradley the only mayor to have been criticized for foreign travel. Mayor David Dinkins of New York has often been taken to task for his trips to South Africa, Israel, Japan, and Western Europe.[13]

Frequently, other groups in the community have mobilized against the international preoccupation of city leaders and the types of policies they have promoted. The local chambers of commerce along with business interests have been particularly strong sources of opposition. The four issues examined here have all been opposed by the private sector to some degree. In certain instances, business efforts have often been supported by higher-level government officials. For example, the U.S. Department of Energy is reported to have awarded a defense contractor—RDA Logicam, located in Virginia—a $550,000 contract to "help lobby Congress and the public against a comprehensive test ban treaty."[14]

Due to the potential costs to the nuclear industry, private interests have been very active against the nuclear free zone movement. Earl Molander provides a very illuminating discussion of business response to five communities' efforts to declare themselves NFZs.[15] In the target communities (Cambridge, Massachusetts; Ann Arbor, Michigan; and Santa Cruz, Santa Monica, and Sonoma, California), only a few firms took an active role in the opposition movement with the chamber of commerce leading the opposition in only one case. In all five cases, an independent campaign consultant was hired, and the same firm was employed in three of the cases: Cambridge, Ann Arbor, and Sonoma. For the most part, the opposition firms were defense oriented. There were other supporters, however, including the chamber of commerce in four of the five cases and other firms interested in local economic growth, such as those involved in construction, industrial supply, utility, and waste management.[16]

Business interests were successful in defeating the initiative in all five cases but the cost was not cheap. In the communities where the greatest money was spent by opponents, $796,736 in Cambridge and $384,000 in Sonoma, a no vote was very costly.[17] In Cambridge, the vote was 11,677 (40%) for and 17,331 (60%) against, with the average cost per affirmative vote $2.05 and per no vote a whopping $46. In Sonoma, the vote was 46,316 (40% for and 69,662 (60%) against, with a yes vote costing $2.13 and a no vote $5.50. The extent to which firms were willing to invest in defeating the NFZ initiatives indicates some of the problems economic conversion efforts face as a result of industrial dependency on military-related production and particularly nuclear economics.

The divestment issue has also been opposed by the business community. Two tracks of opposition can be identified. First is the extent to which business departures would address the need for change in the most meaningful way. Many have believed that continued operations in South Africa are more beneficial to blacks than pullouts. Second, there has been concern as to what extent divestment restrictions affect investment portfolio potential. In hearings before a subcommittee of the House Committee on the District of Columbia concerning the district's effort to divest, testimony supporting both views was expressed.[18]

Robert Schwartz, vice president of Shearson American Express, New York, noted that although he did not feel the restrictions were sufficient to limit the earning potential of investment portfolios, American Express and its subsidiary Shearson American Express did not support the divestment concept:

> The companies have corporately expressed an abhorrence to the
> system of apartheid, and believe, however, that a better opposition
> to this system would come from a continued presence in South
> Africa of American companies which attempt in their various fields
> of endeavor to improve the situation of the black population.[19]

He went on to add that American Express supported the Sullivan Principles, a code of conduct for businesses operating in South Africa, although he recognized and stated that there were weaknesses in them.[20]

In regard to the earning potential question, David Eager, director of Meidinger Asset Planning Services, testified on a study conducted by his company for the District of Columbia. The study gathered expert testimony from investment managers and plan supporters around the country to assess the investment implications of the proposed law on the district's three pension funds: teachers, judges, and police and firefighters.[21] Based on their examination of the restricted stock characteristics compared with nonrestricted stocks, Meidinger concluded that the District of Columbia's retirement board should oppose the divestment law:

> We believe that imposing the restrictions of the proposed South Africa law would be detrimental to the investment managers' ability to meet their objectives, would cause the Fund to be more volatile and hold securities of lower overall quality, could reduce future Fund performance and, consequently, cause the District to have to increase contributions (taxes) and/or reduce its ability to improve benefits in the future.[22]

Similar views supporting the contention that companies could have more positive effects if they stayed in South Africa were expressed in response to the state of California's divestiture bill. It was thought that IBM would be the company most affected by the bill, with pension fund investments at about $742 million. IBM spokesman Rich Coyle stated, "We're sorry to lose shareholders, but we have said we will continue to do business there as long as it makes good business sense and we can help people to make positive change in that country."[23] The public relations manager for Tenneco Inc., which had a $238 million investment from California state pension funds, echoed the potential advantage of continued involvement. Charles Schneider said, "We feel our presence there is of benefit to the black community. We have no intention at this time of changing that."[24]

Many businesses clung to the adoption of the Sullivan Principles to justify their continued involvement in South Africa in the 1980s. This argument lost its weight in 1987, however, when the author of this code of conduct, the Reverend Leon Sullivan, a civil rights activist, declared that the principles had "failed to undermine apartheid."[25] Despite adherence to the doctrine by 127 of the approximately 200 businesses operating in South Africa at the time, Sullivan felt they had not achieved meaningful reforms and called for the withdrawal of all business/commercial ties to South Africa. He also called for stronger U.S. action than the sanctions legislation, urging a U.S. embargo on trade to South Africa and calling on President Reagan to sever diplomatic ties with that country.

Business opposition to the sanctuary movement has not been very strong due to the minor impact it projects on commercial interests. What opposition that has been manifested has come from chambers of commerce and government officials fearing an influx of immigrants and potential growth of unemployment as a result of such declarations. Former Governor Richard Lamm of Colorado voiced this concern on the television news program *Nightline,* arguing that sanctuary declarations are a "megaphone" that says "come here" to the rest of the world; export your unemployment to the United States.[26] Such consequences have not been felt to the degree feared, however, given the few people affected by these declarations and the positive benefit they are able to give in certain areas of the economy.[27]

In terms of state responses, Governor Lamm has been one of few governors who have not been supportive of local foreign policy agendas. For the most part, states have been so busy with their own foreign policy agendas that they have given little consideration, beyond benign support, to local activism. Governors and their various lobby organizations, such as the National Conference of Governors (NCG), have actively promoted state actions in the international arena, although the greatest effort has been concentrated on economic issues. They have also been more willing to play by the rules, as they are more likely to consult with sources at the federal level, either through such organizations as the NCG or directly on their own before venturing into foreign policy issues. Many federal governmental agencies also have offices to consult with state-level officials on their activities, particularly in regard to trade, such as the Department of Commerce's Office of Intergovernmental Affairs.

Federal Responses to Local Activism

The federal government under the Reagan and Bush administrations did not encourage local political activism and in several cases was outspoken on its intolerance. While an extreme interpretation might be the fomenting of separatist movements as a result of local activism, Ivo Duchacek notes that national fear revolves around the primary concern that "too many subnational initiatives abroad may lead to chaotic fragmentation and so invite foreign meddling or cause a nation to speak with stridently conflicting voices on the international scene."[28] More generally, based on interviews he conducted with various national elites, Duchacek defined seven sources of central opposition to what he called "subnational microdiplomacy." They can be summarized as follows:

1. Opposition in principle
2. Fear of anything novel
3. Devotion to neatness
4. Fear of consequences resulting from inexperience
5. Fear of political-administrative chaos
6. Fear of subnational egocentrism
7. Fear of a secessionist potential[29]

Many of these same feelings have manifested themselves in regard to the issues examined here. While all of these concerns have been voiced in some capacity, with the exception of a fear of a secessionist potential most particularly rooted in Canadian-Quebec observations, three sources are particularly strong for these issues and to some extent encompass Duchacek's other considerations as well.

Fundamentally, opposition in principle has been a critical element of federal response and offers perhaps the strongest foundation for national opposition. Constitutional principles have frequently been invoked that suggest local activism violates the "eminent domain of national foreign policy."[30] In his discussion of this source of resistance, Duchacek wryly notes that " 'a single legitimate voice abroad' was after all, what the Constitutional Convention of 1787 was partly about."[31] Legal arguments revolving around constitutional provisions in particular have been advanced in this regard. The arguments that have been raised offer substantial opposition and will be discussed more thoroughly below.

Beyond legal objections is the fear of inadvertent consequences resulting from local inexperience in regard to particularly sensitive issues. It is possible that local actions undertaken without proper authority may create political misunderstandings for federal officials. It could be argued that Duchacek's identification of government officials' fear of anything novel contributes to this concern. The commitment to procedure and the federal government's need for control in foreign policy issues support this rationale.

A third consideration that leads from inadvertent consequences is the fear of political-administrative chaos. Again, this concern emerges from a legal basis. Howard N. Fenton, a former official with the International Trade Administration of the Commerce Department, echoes these fears in regard to local divestment sanctions.[32] He believes these actions serve as "powerful counterweights" to federal policies and as a result "the U.S. ends up with hundreds of foreign policies rather than one." Underlying this argument is the devotion to neatness Duchacek identifies as an additional source of national uneasiness. A similar rationale can be advanced for Duchacek's fear of subnational egocentrism as local governments ignore federal foreign policy directives and pursue their own perceptions and actions on the issues.

State Department legal assistant Peter Spiro draws comparable distinctions that reinforce these arguments. Writing for the conservative journal *Washington Quarterly*, Spiro offers a strong case against local foreign policy.[33] He is particularly concerned that certain types of actions pose a serious challenge to federal initiative and responsibility, especially in regard to national security issues. He believes such actions are "not appropriate" for the U.S. system of federalism. He offers three points of opposition: (a) most states and cities are ill-suited to the task, (b) local foreign policy gives active cities a power beyond their equal vote in the federal system, and (c) the potency of widespread local action gives rise to federal powerlessness. At best, local measures dilute federal policy; at worst, they render federal action ineffectual.[34] To combat the encroachment of these activities on national security, Spiro is particularly supportive of legal arguments.

Local Initiatives:
A Violation of U.S. Law?

Local foreign policy opponents have found strong legal arguments that bolster their position. Despite rulings and opinions to the contrary, the federal government has continued to believe legal recourse is available if cities go too far in their foreign policy initiatives. The basis for their arguments revolves around two constitutional provisions (the Supremacy Clause and the Commerce Clause) and one case precedent (*Zschernig v. Miller*).[35]

The constitutional arguments are based on the exclusive powers of the federal system relative to state and local interests. The Supremacy Clause is detailed in Article VI of the Constitution and simply asserts that the Constitution and all laws made in pursuance of it are to be the supreme law of the land. Subsequent interpretation of this article has led to the formulation of the preemption doctrine, which gives federal law supremacy over state and local statutes; to the extent to which they are in conflict with federal law, it preempts them. Similar concerns are expressed in the Commerce Clause, detailed in Article I, Section 8. Generally, this section is concerned with enumerating the various powers of Congress, including the power to regulate commerce not only with foreign nations but among states as well.[36]

These clauses come into effect in regard to local foreign policy issues when such actions are deemed outside federal parameters. The preemption doctrine has been given careful consideration in regard to the divestment and sanctuary issues but only limited action has been taken.[37] The hearings on the Washington, D.C., divestment action were one effort to delineate federal and local responsibility in this regard; however, the proposed resolution to stop the effort was not supported. The District of Columbia case is peculiar in this regard because of the Home Rule Act, which established the district's authority distinct from the federal government. The hearings not only considered the constitutionality of the action and whether it obstructed federal interest but were also concerned with whether the district's council had exceeded its mandate. Similar questions were raised with the congressional passage of the Sanctions Bill in 1986. The House passed a resolution that stated that the bill would not preempt state and local actions; however, it was not a part of the sanctions act and as such was not an enforceable law.[38]

The federal government decided to lift economic sanctions against South Africa in July 1991 and has been unhappy with the decision of local communities not to follow suit. This dissatisfaction was strong enough for Herman Cohen, assistant secretary of state for African affairs, to warn that the Justice Department was considering a lawsuit in regard to "the legal implications of states and local governments carrying out their own foreign policy with regard to South Africa," shortly after the sanctions were lifted.[39] This was not the first time legal action has been suggested or pursued in regard to local divestment activities. A case came before the Maryland Supreme Court in 1989 questioning a Baltimore ordinance that prohibited city investment in firms doing business in South Africa. While the court upheld the city's right, it did so only in the context that the action from the court's view had "minimal and indirect" influence on South Africa.[40]

Both the preemption doctrine and the Commerce Clause have been cited as possible legal recourses to nuclear free zone declarations. In invoking the preemption doctrine, a memo from Draper Labs, the primary target of the Cambridge campaign and a major opponent of the NFZ movement, argued against the free zone declarations on the following grounds:

First, the proposed initiative would be invalid . . . because its subject matter is "preempted" by federal legislation with which it would conflict; in addition, it seeks to affect areas of exclusive federal concern. Cambridge has no power to cancel or subvert federal defense policy, even if Cambridge residents would prefer a different policy.[41]

The Draper memo also suggested the proposed action would infringe on the freedom of speech and inquiry rights of company employees involved in the research and development of nuclear weapons.

In regard to the Commerce Clause, the argument is that the nuclear free zone designation may hamper the free flow of interstate commerce in regard to nuclear-related products. In one of the few legal opinions expressed in this regard, the city attorney of Portland, Oregon, Christopher Thomas, has argued the burden would be slight.[42]

Both arguments were used in 1990 when the Nuclear Free Zone movement suffered a setback as one of the toughest nuclear free zone initiatives passed by the city of Oakland was stripped of its power by a U.S. district court. The suit was brought by the U.S. Justice Department against the city of Oakland, challenging the constitutionality of the ordinance. The case came before Reagan-appointed federal judge J. P. Vukasin, who had been a college roommate of Edwin Meese, the attorney general during Reagan's second term in office.[43] Vukasin supported the government's claim that the War Powers Clause and the Supremacy Clause of the Constitution along with the Atomic Energy Act and the Hazardous Materials Transportation Act preempted the Oakland ordinance. The result was that the ordinance was stripped of all but the power to post signs at the city limits declaring itself a nuclear free zone with no means of enforcement. The city council decided not to appeal the written opinion that had rejected the ordinance as "invalid on its face," which resulted in it being thrown out without a trial. They did, however, redraft the measure and passed it in June 1992. It has not been challenged to date.

The third legal argument against local activism and perhaps the strongest is the Supreme Court finding in the 1968 case of *Zschernig v. Miller*.[44] The facts of the case are as follows: The state of Oregon passed an ordinance that provided that certain requirements be met in the inheritance of land by foreign heirs. Specifically, the case involved property left by an Oregon resident to his only heirs who resided in the former East Germany. The Oregon statute prohibited this inheritance on the basis that the former East Germany did not allow U.S. residents to inherit property; there were no reciprocal rights for U.S. citizens.[45] The Supreme Court debated the legitimacy of the Oregon statute and found it to be an intrusion into the foreign policy powers of the federal government as mandated by the Constitution. In the opinion of the Court as written by Justice Douglas:

> The present Oregon law . . . has a direct impact upon foreign relations and may well adversely affect the power of the central government to deal with those problems. The Oregon law does, indeed, illustrate the dangers which are involved if each State, speaking through its probate courts, is permitted to establish its own foreign policy.[46]

The decision in *Zschernig v. Miller* gives the federal government a strong precedent to act on the legality of local foreign policy actions. To this date, however, local actions have not been deemed dangerous enough to warrant direct action using this precedent against them. This does not preclude that alternative, and the fact that people such as Spiro at the State Department have vigorously researched points of legal opposition may ultimately lead to confrontation. Lee Hunt, legislative management officer in the State Department's Office of Legislative and Intergovernmental Affairs, observed that while many local actions on foreign policy issues are just feel-good resolutions that benefit local leaders in the eyes of their activist constituents, they could be subject to judicial challenge but are let go.[47] She cited the preemption doctrine and interstate commerce regulation as grounds for legal action, noting that many actions come "dangerously close to unconstitutionality." Nevertheless, because they have little effect beyond the local level from their perspective, no direct charges have been leveled. The exception to this observation is the case of the sanctuary movement.

The sanctuary movement has suffered the greatest legal setbacks with the 1986 criminal trial of 11 Tucson activists accused of conspiracy and smuggling in the aid of Salvadoran and Guatemalan refugees fleeing their homelands. Felony charges were leveled against the church-based movement after an undercover Immigration and Naturalization Service investigation. A total of 8 of the 11 activists were called to trial, including a Presbyterian minister, two Roman Catholic priests, and a nun, and were convicted on various charges and given probationary sentences of varying lengths.[48] The initial decision to prosecute the case was critical to the growth of the sanctuary movement. Although many have argued that the guilty verdicts were the "death knell for the sanctuary movement," according to Donald M. Reno, a special assistant U.S. attorney, activist supporters contend the opposite has occurred.[49]

As can be seen from this discussion, legal arguments have not been used extensively to prohibit local activism, despite their potential strength. While the machinery is available through the law and case precedent, the cost has been evaluated to be just too high for the benefits gained. The ill will that is invoked by legal recourse is not regained in the minor impact on local activism.

Relative Successes

Despite objections from the community and the federal government, the achievements of local foreign policy activism have been significant at all levels of analysis. Expanding on the expressive versus instrumental distinctions outlined at the outset, various measures of success can be offered to evaluate accomplishments at the local, national, and international levels. Expressive measures include the extent to which public debate has been generated on a given issue. The emergence of foreign policy issues in local campaigns, the passage of nonbinding resolutions, the development of educational efforts, the establishment of friendship ties, and the development of lobbying concerns are all examples of this trend. This increased awareness has frequently led to more tangible returns. In that regard, instrumental measures range from structural changes that institutionalize local activism to amending various policy outcomes at higher levels of government. For example, more than 10 cities have established their own offices of international affairs, while commissions to study the impact of military spending have been established in several cities.[50] These developments emphasize the strength of the local foreign policy movement and the successes they have enjoyed.

In regard to the four issues examined here, both expressive and instrumental successes have been realized. While the comprehensive test ban movement is essentially an expressive type of action at the local level, proponents argue their efforts were critical to the negotiation of the INF treaty and Strategic Arms Reduction Treaty (SALT) talks. They believe the public support that grew out of the nuclear freeze movement and now manifests itself in the comprehensive test ban resolutions was a prime motivator to the Reagan administration to bring about some limits to nuclear weapons production.

During the Bush administration, the test ban movement finally gained the serious attention of Congress in August 1992. The Senate passed an amendment (68 to 26), sponsored by Senator Mark Hatfield (R-OR), to impose a moratorium on U.S. nuclear testing until July 1993. The amendment also provided for a ban on nuclear testing after September 10, 1996, unless a former USSR republic conducted a nuclear test in that period; this was later extended to any foreign state. A similar measure passed the House of Representatives on September 24, 1992, sponsored by Representative Les Aspin (D-WI). Aspin would later become the secretary of defense in the Clinton administration.

The White House became involved with this issue following the Bush administration as a result of President Clinton's personal commitment to a permanent ban. Just two days after the congressional moratorium expired, Clinton ordered the moratorium to be extended for an additional 15 months. In a radio address to the American people on July 3, 1993, Clinton called on other nuclear powers to join the United States in this test ban. He also noted, however, that the United States would "move quickly to conduct additional tests" should any other country resume testing before the proposed October 1994 deadline.[51]

The growth of nuclear free zones has been successful on several levels. Not only have they stated a public preference for a community free from nuclear weapons and related industries but, in almost half of the cities that have passed declarations to date, there are legally binding limitations as well. As noted earlier, NFZs have elicited a strong business lobby, which has spent exorbitant amounts of money to prevent their passage. The fact that business fears are so great is a measure of success in and of itself. The public attention that is generated by such activities alone makes such efforts worthwhile.

Divestment actions have been the most successful in eliciting a national policy response in the form of sanctions legislation. They have also involved tangible resources, resulting in the withdrawal of more than $20 billion in public funds from businesses operating in South Africa, according to the American Committee on Africa (ACOA). Furthermore, the Investor Responsibility Research Center (IRRC) has calculated the cost to the South African economy based on these sanctions to be $27 billion.[52] The state of California alone made a tremendous impact on these figures, accounting for $7.2 billion in public, teacher, and University of California employee pension funds that were divested by the end of 1990.[53]

In addition, Reverend Sullivan's condemnation of the Sullivan Principles coupled with these withdrawals prompted the pullout of several major corporations from that market, ranging from food-service companies such as Kentucky Fried Chicken to major automobile companies such as Ford and General Motors. While some of the corporate withdrawals have not represented a total severing of ties to South Africa, because many of them have simply sold their holdings to their subsidiaries, the movement still represents a shift of resources as a result of an active lobby effort and pressure to bring about meaningful change.

Even with the Bush administration's decision to lift sanctions in July 1991, most local efforts have stood fast. Although South African diplomats have urged the reversal of these policies, formerly jailed ANC leader Nelson Mandela, who many believe was released because of these local efforts, has asked that they be kept in place until meaningful transition toward a new government has been made.

The sanctuary issue represents the most controversial action of local governments, as it directly advocates disobeying federal authority, specifically the INS. The adversarial nature of this effort has led many cities to pass resolutions in support of Salvadoran or Gautemalan refugees without the actual declaration of sanctuary. Santa Monica, California, has passed a resolution to this effect, and the case of Los Angeles addressed in the previous discussion illustrates some of the pitfalls. There has been progress in dealing with the problems of El Salvador and Guatemala. The elections and peace accords in El Salvador have been heralded by the United States as bringing about great change in that country. From the activists' point of view, however, the jury is still out.

What Accounts for These Successes?

What are the factors that can be attributed to these relative successes? The answer lies in the four agents identified to explain these behaviors at the outset: public opinion, interest groups, the cities themselves, and the system within which they operate. Many of these local successes have depended on cyclical variations in public attentiveness. The extent to which the public is moved to act on an issue, either by interest groups, the media, or national and international events, may be crucial to the success of local activism on a given issue. For example, the growing fear of a nuclear holocaust around the world has been critical to the growth of the test ban and free zone movements.

An expanding citizenship agenda is emerging that includes foreign affairs. Citizens exercising their democratic freedoms seek influence in the international system because it increasingly affects their daily lives. Unwilling to follow presidential initiatives, they have struck out on their own, as popular support for the way the president is handling key foreign policy issues has dwindled. The chief executive no longer enjoys the public support that has traditionally structured public opinion on foreign affairs.

Constituency demands are broadening with their new awareness. In his discussion of cultural pressures on the nation-state, Seyom Brown argues that a growing identification of American blacks with their African roots has been the impetus for action against the apartheid regime of South Africa.[54] He goes on to suggest that congressional overturning of President Reagan's veto of the sanction's bill was a reflection of congressional interest in their black constituents:

> The sanctions against the South African government by the American Congress in 1986, over the veto of President Reagan, was not simply an expression of popular American sentiment on human rights. It was by many, including the majority of members of Congress from the president's own party, the product of the practical realization that the South African issue is highly salient for the blacks in their constituencies and, moreover, that the black political leadership is now in a position to swing the election in many key districts against

candidates who cross them on this issue, and might even be able to determine the outcome of senatorial and presidential elections.[55]

If this observation is indeed accurate, the newly mobilized black and supportive minority constituency may become a more critical force in national politics.

A second source for this citizen activism is the Vietnam War and the fragmentation of loyalties that emerged. Vietnam forced people to speak out on a foreign policy issue, to take a stand in conflict with national leadership. The horror of the war was brought home through the television medium.[56] The cold war mentality, which sustained a generation, was brought into question as the United States failed in its objectives.

Brown notes that the youth counterculture that emerged in the 1960s in opposition to the Vietnam War has new followers today. The youths of today no longer direct their anger toward the system; instead their anger is focused on specific issues like the ones considered here. Brown bases the explanation for such behavior on an erosion of confidence in authority: "The accelerating rate of scientific, technological, and socioeconomic change is disrupting allegiance to traditional influences; and faith is waning that the traditional authority does indeed retain command of significant knowledge, resources, and groups of people."[57] With this lack of confidence, the age of mobility has exacerbated the decline of community cohesion and respect for legitimate power sources. New avenues of expression are sought. As Brown notes, "Bases of community other than the nation-state are increasingly vying for the affection and loyalty of individuals."[58] The result is the middle-class radicalism, observed by Mark Kann and others in city politics, that has contributed to the development of local foreign policy activism.

This changing public mood has been capitalized on by activist and interest groups faced with failures at the national level that are seeking alternative avenues of expression. Public opinion has been receptive to these broader agendas but generally passive without the stimulation of interest groups or simple active and interested individuals. Interest groups justify their local activism as responsiveness to these public demands. Capitalizing on federal frustration, local groups have formed to develop agendas that build on public mood, democratic expression, and growing global consciousness.

The organizational strength of activist groups behind the issues, however, continues to be a prime factor in the attention various issues have received. For example, in the primarily military-dependent city of San Diego, California, economic conversion became an issue in city council elections due to the activities of the San Diego Economic Conversion Council.[59] The group raised the issue as part of its "educational efforts" by asking all candidates to respond to a questionnaire that explored the impact of military spending on the city. Seven of the eight candidates responded, with six of those seven favorably responsive to the notion that military dependency could be a problem for San Diego's long-term economic well-being. Since the election, two of the winners have voiced support for the exploration of economic alternatives to reduce the impact of military spending on the city. Recent cuts and military base closures reinforce the importance of seeking viable solutions.

Another source of explanation is found in the types of cities that have acted on these issues. There are many similarities among the cities that have acted on specific issues and those that have been most active generally on all four issues. The progressive radical image emerging in many large urban areas, as noted by Kann, Clavel, and others, goes hand in hand with local activism. The fact that middle-class radicals characterize the constituencies of these areas fits nicely with the Vietnam fragmentation thesis, and the fact that there are large black constituencies in cities active on South Africa supports the cultural awareness and affinity thesis put forth by Brown. Similar conclusions can be drawn concerning Hispanic populations and their support for Central American activism and the sanctuary movement.

A final explanation lies in the system in which cities operate and the effects their actions may have at the national and international levels. The shrinking nature of the international system and expanding level of interaction citizens can now enjoy with people all over the world have certainly given impetus to the growing awareness the public now possesses. Feeling remote to the federal

governing apparatus and often closer to the plight of citizens around
the world, citizens have been moved to act beyond their boundaries and outside traditional channels to voice their concerns.

Consequences at the
National and International Levels

What then are the consequences of local activism? Do these
actions represent an erosion of U.S. foreign policy goals abroad?
Is there a potential conflict in terms of political administrative
authority that might result in inadvertent consequences from local
activism on sensitive issues?

The answers to these questions are not easily measured or dis-
cerned. Duchacek observes that the limitations of experimenta-
tion in the realm of international relations are such that it is not
possible to reproduce actions in a closed environment to measure
various outcomes as is possible in the hard sciences.[60] Nevertheless, it is possible to speculate about what consequences may
result. The fact that the federal government has taken only limited
actions given the legal recourses available to it suggests a tolerance
for local activism. Also, the extent to which national policies have
been modified, as noted in the discussion of relative successes,
indicates a positive benefit for local foreign policy to its proponents. While these actions may suggest a potential fear for opponents
to local foreign policy, it has not been great enough to warrant
truly limiting actions.

The question remains, however, about the future of these activities. Many would argue the growth of municipal foreign policy
was a 1980s phenomenon, influenced by the nature of the national political administration and the changing international system
that forced the community into the world beyond. Yet cities have
clung to the policies they have adopted, mayors continue to travel
abroad, sister city relationships have flourished, and interest
groups have not disbanded. Will the 1990s see a new direction in
these activities?

Notes

1. Shuman, M. H. (1987). *Building municipal foreign policies: An action handbook*. Irvine, CA: The Center for Innovative Diplomacy's Local Elected Officials Project; and Spiro, P. J. (1988). Taking foreign policy away from the feds. *Washington Quarterly, 11,* 191-203.

2. Shuman (1987, pp. 22-30).

3. Spiro (1988).

4. Spiro (1988, p. 194).

5. This distinction was pointed out to me by James N. Rosenau, George Washington University.

6. The following comments were taken from a lecture and question-and-answer period by Richard Alatorre given as part of the fifth annual Chicano Studies Lecture Series at Loyola Marymount University in Los Angeles on April 11, 1988.

7. Merina, V. (1985, November 28). Council votes 8-6 for L.A. sanctuary. *Los Angeles Times,* sec. 1, p. 1; and Merina, V. (1986, February 8). L.A. council backs down on sanctuary plan. *Los Angeles Times,* sec. 1, p. 1.

8. Merina (1986).

9. Quoted in Merina (1986, p. 1).

10. San Buenaventura, California. (1971, May 18). *A resolution of the city council of the city of San Buenaventura stating its position on national and international policies and affairs.* Resolution No. 7227.

11. Bunting, G. F. (1990, September 30). Bradley's foreign travels top all big-city mayors. *Los Angeles Times,* sec. A, p. 1.

12. Boyarsky, B. (1992, March 21). Send out a search party—Our mayor is missing. *Los Angeles Times,* sec. B, p. 1.

13. McKinley, Jr., J. C. (1991, October 12). Angry Dinkins defends travel to South Africa. *New York Times,* sec. 1, p. 33.

14. Shuman, M. H. (1987-1988). Ban nuclear testing. *Bulletin of Municipal Foreign Policy, 2,* 2.

15. Molander, E. A. (1987, September). *Business response and responsibility in the issue of nuclear free zones.* Paper presented at the 1987 American Political Science Association Convention, Chicago.

16. Molander (1987).

17. Molander (1987).

18. U.S. Congress, House, Committee on the District of Columbia. (1984). *South Africa Divestment, Hearings before a subcommittee on fiscal affairs and health of the House Commmittee on the District of Columbia,* 98th Cong., 2nd sess. These hearings considered two House resolutions introduced by Representative Crane that sought to stop the District of Columbia's divestment actions as a violation of its charter. It is important to note that there was testimony that disagreed with these points as well. In the end, however, the resolutions were rejected by the committee.

19. U.S. Congress (1984, p. 166).

20. U.S. Congress (1984).

21. U.S. Congress (1984).

22. U.S. Congress (1984, p. 139).

23. Paddock, R. C. (1986, September 27). Governor signs South Africa divestiture bill. *Los Angeles Times,* sec. 1, pp. 1, 35. Quotes from this article are used with permission.

24. Paddock (1986, p. 35).

25. Sullivan asks end of business links with South Africa. (1987, June 4). *New York Times,* sec. 1, p. 1.

26. ABC. (1986, April 1). *Nightline.*

27. Economic advisers see positive contribution by illegal aliens. (1986, February 7). *Los Angeles Times,* sec. 1, p. 13.

28. Duchacek, I. D. (1986). *The territorial dimension of politics: Within, among, and across nations.* Boulder, CO: Westview.

29. Duchacek, I. D. (1984). The international dimension of subnational self-government. *Publius: The Journal of Federalism, 14,* 20-22. Barber offers similar arguments against citizen participation in urban politics generally in Barber, D. M. (1981). *Citizen participation in American communities: Strategies for success.* Dubuque, IA: Kendall/Hunt.

30. Duchacek (1986, p. 249).

31. Duchacek (1986, p. 249).

32. Fenton, H. N. (1990, March 30). Repeal local divestment sanctions. *Christian Science Monitor,* p. 18.

33. Spiro (1988).

34. Spiro (1988).

35. For a good discussion of the legal issues, see Shuman, M. H. (1992). Dateline main street: Courts v. local foreign policies. *Foreign Policy, 86,* 158-177.

36. The Commerce Clause has been broadly construed in several cases, most notably as a rationale against discrimination in public accomodations (hotels, restaurants, etc.).

37. For a legal discussion of preemption and sanctuary declarations see McMillan, D. D. (1987). City sanctuary resolutions and the preemption doctrine: *Much ado about nothing. Loyola of Los Angeles Law Review, 20,* 513-572.

38. An interesting discussion of the potential legal limitations that could arise in this regard is offered by Smith, G. A. (1987, March 16). Apartheid act casts doubt on local laws. *Los Angeles Times,* sec. 2, p. 5.

39. Shuman (1992, p. 159).

40. Shuman (1992, p. 160).

41. Molander (1987, p. 12).

42. Shuman (1987).

43. Rauber, P. (1990, June 11). Zoned nuke-free. *The Nation,* p. 826.

44. Friedmann, W., Lissitzyn, O. J., & Pugh, R. C. (1969). *International law: Cases and materials.* St. Paul, MN: West. A previous ruling was made in this regard in the 1947 case of *Clark v. Allen.* The circumstances were similar, but in this case, the Court upheld the California State statute, arguing it had only an "incidental or indirect effect" on U.S. foreign policy. See Shuman (1987, pp. 34-35) for a more thorough discussion of the relationship between these two cases.

45. The statute was a reflection of the cold war mentality at the time and was an effort to chastise communist countries.

46. Friedmann, Lissitzyn, & Pugh (1969, p. 135).

47. Interview with Lee Hunt, April 17, 1987.

48. Despite prosecutions, sanctuary movement is still vital, growing, its activists insist. (1987, July 11). *Los Angeles Times* sec. 2, p. 5.

49. "Despite Prosecutions" (1987).

50. Davis examines impact of military spending. (1987-1988). *Bulletin of Municipal Foreign Policy, 2,* 27; Baltimore advisory committee gears up for action. (1987-1988). *Bulletin of Municipal Foreign Policy, 2,* 27; and Shuman (1992).

51. Jehl, D. (1993, July 4). Clinton urges other nuclear powers to join U.S. in a moratorium on testing. *New York Times,* sec. 1, p. 4.

52. The last mile: U.S. communities and South Africa. (1991-1992, Winter). *Global Communities,* p. 2.

53. Morain, D. (1990, July 1). Divestment forces say pressure paid off. *Los Angeles Times,* sec. A, p. 3.

54. Brown, S. (1988). *New forces, old forces and the future of world politics.* Glenview, IL: Scott, Foresman.

55. Brown (1988).

56. It is interesting to note that media coverage of military actions is now limited. Films of the Gulf War were restricted, and films of the U.S. invasion of Grenada were made by the military itself. Journalists were kept out "for their own safety." Similarly, the UK provided films of its invasion of the Falkland and Malvinas Islands.

57. Brown (1988, p. 210).

58. Brown (1988, p. 211).

59. Conversion issue raised in San Diego mayoral election. (1987-1988). *Bulletin of Municipal Foreign Policy, 2,* 28.

60. Duchacek (1984).

5

Whither Municipal Foreign Policy?

All of the issues reviewed here—comprehensive test ban, nuclear free zones, divestment, and sanctuary—have generated both a national and local focus. Today, these issues are victims of their own successes: The so-called end of the cold war has rendered nuclear issues less pressing, many believe change is eminent in South Africa, and the peace accords with El Salvador are moving on track by many observers estimates. Yet where have all the activists gone? What has happened to the organizations that so fervently pursued these causes in the 1980s? What is the future of municipal foreign policy? Will the movement be renewed under the Clinton administration or will the activists' attention turn to other areas?

Across the United States today, public opinion has shifted inward with an overarching concern with domestic, particularly economic, problems. The groups involved in these issues remain active but their interests and agendas have been refocused. Cities have increasingly been pushed to redirect their energies locally and forget a broader political agenda. Increasingly, Main Street America has decided to stay home in the 1990s with regard to political issues. What international contact that has been sanctioned has focused on the area of trade and foreign investment in the hope for international economic solutions to local fiscal problems.

Even Santa Monica, California, the archetype for middle-class radicalism has fallen to the recession, experiencing a deficit in 1992, the first in 20 years.[1] The result has been a reduction of tax-supported services by $5.7 million, elimination of 60 city jobs through attrition, and a 1% cut in social services. The mayor has also joined in, motivated by reelection concerns, and voted to cut his travel budget by almost 50%.

Many believe citizen activism is just not a viable force in the 1990s. Montgomery County, just outside of Washington, D.C., has had one of the most successful civic activist movements since the 1940s.[2] Things have changed for this group in recent years, however, as the suburbs within the county want to act in their own interests. Furthermore, women, the backbone of the movement through the years, have taken careers, including political office, and no longer have the time to devote to civic issues. Despite an increased minority population in the community, the movement remains middle class and is essentially focused on property values. Often the county and developers simply do not listen to the concerns of the group and are responsive only when a lawyer is engaged on a specific concern. Some critics suggest the past successes of the group in adding citizen advisory groups and zoning reforms that now characterize county government have left the activists with little else to do. All of these factors have resulted in a loss of power for the group generally. Its supporters are not giving up; they simply no longer have the clout they once enjoyed.

A similar circumstance has occurred in Los Angeles. While Los Angeles never pretended to be particularly responsive to civic activism as the city council tended to act in a trusteeship role, there was the illusion of receptivity to the diverse population. Davis argues that this responsiveness has been a hoax by the city government, which has exploited the community. He suggests that some representatives have, in fact, used community protest for their own gain. In particular, he cites council members who have reaped larger campaign contributions from developers by supporting local protests against development. The result has been community alienation from their representatives. In the aftermath of the L.A. riots and fires, the effort to rebuild has exacerbated these divisions. Davis believes the only viable solution is a genuine return to the community through elected neighborhood governments. Only then will grassroots movements be taken seriously and real progress be made toward resolving conflicts. He concludes that citizens who bridge their efforts toward conflict resolution have more to gain in the future than those who profit from dissent.[4]

Despite these shortcomings, there is still support for citizen activism. Walls argues that such organizations are "the key to social change."[5] While he concedes that they may have their problems, nevertheless, they are essential to political life in the 1990s. He agrees that the trends that have been examined here—the development of a postindustrial society, the decline of the manufacturing North in favor of the service-oriented South, and the international revolution that has fundamentally changed the structure of relations among nations—underlie city activism, or as he argues, "generate structures of political opportunity for social movements."[6] He is optimistic about the future of citizen activism and provides a guide to what he defines as the "leading advocacy organizations in America," encouraging citizen participation.

Where Have All the Activists Gone?

To survive in today's world, activist movements have redirected their energies based on both their activities and the changing national and international climate surrounding them. These changes reflect a growing attention to environmental concerns, the increasing federal responsiveness to some of the issues, and the international successes they have achieved through their efforts. A survey of the current agendas of the interest groups that have been active on the issues studied here details these new directions.

The Nuclear Weapons Freeze Campaign (NWFC) and the Committee for a SANE Nuclear Policy merged in 1987 to take advantage of the national identity SANE enjoyed and the local chapters and the numerous local units organized by the NWFC. The merged group has renamed itself "Peace Action," with the additional tagline "for a SANE world" to indicate their continued association with the long-standing (since 1957) SANE organization. The change in name reflects the new campaign adopted by the organization. Their overall political goal remains one of commitment to public education on nuclear issues at all levels. Specifically, their priorities are directed in three areas.[7]

The first concern is the promotion of a peace economy. The objective here is to reorient U.S. government budget priorities to cut military spending and move toward human needs. They are particularly interested in economic conversion. They would like to see not only federal legislation in this area but state and local planning institutions and processes as well.

The second priority is nuclear disarmament and nonproliferation. The comprehensive test ban remains the cornerstone of this objective, emphasizing public education with lobby attention now focused on the federal government. They have not neglected local action, however; Peace Action offers the *CTB Education Action Kit* for $5, which includes "everything an activist needs to know about nuclear testing: history, legislative language, 'safety and reliability' facts, sample letters and more."[8] Overall, according to Burt Glass, they believe they have been successful in the test ban area. Their strategy has developed with the times.

> Back in the early 1980s, the federal government wasn't listening. Activists were looking for a way to force the issue on the federal government by local action. Now the federal government is more attentive. The people in Congress cut their teeth on these issues. They have now passed a law on nuclear testing. We are now focusing on the new administration.[9]

The decision by President Clinton to extend the moratorium supports this strategy and suggests a more sympathetic ear in the White House.

In the area of nuclear disarmament and nonproliferation, the group also supports tightening export controls on the spread of nuclear technology. They continue to drive for total nuclear disarmament, which they believe is possible and urge ratification of the START II treaty as a step toward this end.

The third priority, putting an end to arms transfers, is the newest objective and is just more than 1 year old. According to Glass, the focus here is on U.S. sales of conventional weapons.

> The U.S. is the number one arms trader with over 57% of arms sold last year globally by the U.S. Many of these weapons are going to unstable regions which are not democratic. The weapons we sell have been pointed back at us, as in the Gulf War. We have to keep high budgets due to the threat from the third world that we have armed.[10]

While federal lobbying remains the major way to promote this objective, secondary priorities toward achieving this goal include education not only of the public about the arms trade but, even more important, of members within the organization. The International Office of Peace Action has prepared a monograph, *Arms Trade Reader,* and companion video to be distributed to regional affiliates.[11]

Generally, the nuclear freeze movement remains strong within its newly defined existence. It acknowledges it has been weakened by the end of the cold war, but Glass notes they have now "institutionalized the movement. . . . And we have staff to move ahead on critical issues."[12] Their ability to redirect their energies as outlined in their new priorities will define that success.

The nuclear free zone movement has faced some of the problems that the freeze activists have encountered. They experienced a lull due to the end of the cold war and had to rethink their approach. They were forced to stop publishing their newsletter 2 years ago and had to retrench financially to survive. In the past, their position was based on opposition to nuclear weapons and power proliferation. Now, according to Chuck Johnson, director of Nuclear Free America, they are including environmental concerns.[13] Specifically, they are dealing with reduction and elimination of radioactive waste, which bridges the gap between the weapons and power focus. They are now circulating a model ordinance that addresses both concerns. They were also hampered by the Oakland case court ruling. Their ability to pass a subsequent version of the ordinance, however, has given them renewed hope.

Another new direction for the movement, in addition to opposition to radioactive waste dumps, has been to encourage the boycott of and divestment from nuclear weapons makers. Nuclear Free America has prepared a very sophisticated study on the performance of investments of nuclear weapons contractors from 1986 to 1991.[14] They found that inclusion of nuclear equities in investment portfolios overall has in fact been a drag on portfolio performance compared with other similar corporations. They argue that the continued decline in defense budget levels will further weaken this investment option.

Divestment advocates argue they have been the most successful of local initiative movements. Positive responses from the South African government with moves toward greater representation of blacks in the government, the release of Nelson Mandela, and legalization of the African National Congress (ANC) strengthen their argument. Despite pending action in some cities questioning the economic consequences of divestment, overall the movement had encountered little opposition. Today, the advocates of divestment believe its objectives will carry over into relationships with a new South Africa.

Despite developments in South Africa and the decision by the Bush administration in July 1991 to lift sanctions, supporters are cautious in urging local communities to lift their divestment actions. Activists argue the conditions of sanction withdrawal have not been completely met. They believe Mandela's response to the U.N. General Assembly on this question in December 1991 should guide policy.[15] Specifically, Mandela urged that sanctions be lifted in phases, with the first phase focusing on people-to-people exchanges, which the United Nations has supported. The second phase would come with the government ratification of a new constitution and the transfer of power to an interim administration. It is at this point that the lifting of all state and local sanctions would apply, according to the American Committee on Africa (ACOA) and TransAfrica. The third phase of lifting sanctions would come with the election of a new majority government, which would then open the trade ways for arms and oil.

Increasingly, those associated with the movement are trying to look ahead to the next phase of relations with South Africa. As changes are made in South Africa, corresponding changes can be made in the United States, which can assist in South Africa's future. According to Richard Knight, with Africa Fund, an educational division of the ACOA:

> The movement out of South Africa is part of the whole awareness of social responsibility. . . . The ANC is going to want investment done in a socially responsible manner. Blacks couldn't own businesses until a few years ago. The choice is to either go back to the old-fashioned way of doing business or abide by new social responsibility.[16]

Knight credits the social responsibility movement in the United States for tremendous success in bringing about change in South Africa. He now believes that sense of goodwill should carry over to other areas. This is particularly important in the business exchanges that will develop with a new South Africa. Knight believes the progress made to date will be instrumental in this development:

> Social responsibility can play a role by stretching out the hand to business. They want to do business the right way. Social responsibility gives them political cover. Africa Fund and the activists on the issue then become their ally as opposed to enemy.[17]

By remaining committed to a new government for South Africa before any tangible changes will take place, divestment advocates continue to urge fortification of sanctions legislation to ensure their goals are achieved.

The sanctuary movement has encountered the greatest federal opposition. Federal prosecution and sentencing of sanctuary advocates in Tucson, Arizona, stifled the actions of many local communities. Much of sanctuary activism today remains with the churches from which it originated. The sanctuary movement constituted the most direct violation of U.S. federal law, specifically that of INS. It advocated safe passage and asylum for Central American refugees fleeing political persecution in the homelands. Because the United States was friendly with the governments of both El Salvador and Guatemala, from which the majority of refugees were fleeing, they argued the immigrants were economic and not political refugees.

The changing U.S. relationship with El Salvador makes the asylum status for Salvadoran refugees much more difficult. The United States, in cooperation with the U.N., has actively been involved in the repatriation of Central American refugees as the peace accords have been successfully implemented in El Salvador.[18] There are some who would argue, however, that the actions of the U.N. have been overzealous, as the U.N. has also sought repatriation of refugees to Guatemala from Mexico, despite continued political unrest in that country.

Today, what few activities remain under the rubric of sanctuary are residual as opposed to a new wave of activism, according to Darlene Gramena of the Chicago Religious Task Force.[19] While the churches are still active and documentation for refugees is provided through Documentation Exchange, formerly the Central American Resource Center, Gramena believes the Tucson case really divided the movement. "It scared people. The movement was on a path but was slowed down by the trial, by the people on trial who took it personal as opposed to public."[20] She felt that the way in which the defendants proceeded at the trial, by following the rules of the court and engaging their own lawyers, really undermined the unity of the movement. While there has been positive effects from these actions in terms of changes in immigration law to provide broader flexibility to individuals in this regard, as a social movement, it has simply not reached their expectations.[21] As Gramena sums it up, "We had greater hopes of [sanctuary] being a social movement and digging deeper. Instead it was one mile wide and only one inch deep."[22]

Though there is no evidence to suggest that the cities that origin- ally passed sanctuary resolutions have rescinded them, with the exception of Seattle, there has been no new municipal movement on the issue. There is no group keeping track of the movement today. The churches, however, did enjoy a federal ruling in their favor at the end of 1990 that limited the government's authority to secretly observe and tape record church gatherings, the method by which much of the evidence against the Tucson litigants was obtained.[23]

Return to Isolationism?

Does the decline of local activism on these issues suggest a return to isolationism for cities? The argument that things have gotten worse for cities in the 1990s would support such a return; however, if it is examined from an historical perspective, the same problems were there in the 1980s. In fact, during the 1980s, major urban areas experienced some of their greatest setbacks. The Reagan policy of new federalism proved to be an economic disaster for many. This trend, however, had begun much earlier as the history of urban government has detailed.

With the problems they experienced in the postwar era, particularly in the 1980s, cities often welcomed grassroots activity and citizen-based agendas. In some ways, these pursuits distracted the public from the more pressing domestic issues, about which little could be done without significant federal, or as the Reagan and Bush administrations advocated, private intervention. Unfortunately, neither source of support was forthcoming and the foreign policy agendas, while temporarily shifting attention, did not address the endemic problems of the urban areas. Today, these problems have grown more acute and the attraction of international issues, with the exception of foreign trade and investment, is less compelling.

The move away from international issues can be seen in the direction of public opinion over the last few years. Specifically, there has been a significant change in the priority given to various issues in the presidential elections from 1988 to 1992. Just following the elections in 1988, Gallup asked supporters of both President-Elect George Bush and Democratic challenger Michael Dukakis the importance of specific policy issues in their voting choices.[24] In terms of issues, a large percentage (72%) of those polled who voted for Bush believed strengthening defense was very important, exceeded by reducing the drug supply (82%), reducing crime (81%), and improving education (73%). In contrast, only 37% of those who voted for Dukakis believed national defense to be very important. Their most important issue was reducing the drug supply (86%), followed by improving education (84%).

When a similar question was asked by Gallup of all registered voters before the 1992 elections, 93% believed the economy to be very important. Education (87%) and both drugs and crime (77%) remained high on the list. National defense, however, was thought to be very important by only 43% and foreign affairs received the lowest percentage of the issues (37%).[25]

Along with this public shift to more domestic issues and away from foreign policy, other neoisolationist trends in the United States can be observed in the interest in closing the borders to immigrants. Immigration became a hot issue during the 1992 election, fueled by third party candidate Pat Buchanan's outspoken views on stemming immigration from the third world. His view was supported by many Americans; the Gallup Poll found 69% who thought there were too many immigrants from Latin America, 58% believed there were too many from Asia, and 43% believed there were too many from Africa.[26] Job security was also a great fear; 62% of those surveyed agreed with the statement "immigrants take the jobs of U.S. workers." An even larger percentage (64%) believed that many immigrants "wind up on welfare and raise taxes for Americans."

These comments resonate with residents in many areas that have been forced to deal with the problems of immigration locally. Most notably, areas of southern California, particularly San Diego County, have incurred great cost to deal with migrant labor camps and public opposition to them.[27] One city that has been particularly hard hit is Encinitas, California, often called "the flower capital of the world" and a large user of migrant labor. The city declared a state of emergency and billed the federal government almost $300,000 for costs incurred in immigrant-related activities, including cleaning encampments, hiring guards to keep squatters off city land, and establishing a hiring hall for legal day laborers. The federal government declined to pay, however, further fueling community discord with a growing migrant labor population.

The Global Problematique

Cities do not exist in a vacuum. The increasing interdependence of the world and the global problematique of increasing pollution, declining resources, and environmental challenges cannot be ignore. Likewise, international explanations for the growth in local activism, based in the discussion of the decline of the state in its ability to conduct foreign affairs and the growing network of non- state actors in the international arena, cannot be ignored or forgotten.

The communication revolution cannot be turned around; however, it does not necessarily translate to a continued activism on the part of cities in foreign affairs. While the legal threat has perhaps had some small contribution in curtailing these activities, it is minimal. More important, the increased problems of cities and domestic concerns described above are probably a more likely explanation for a decline and refocusing attention to other areas. Unfortunately, the forces that promoted international issues were not as attentive to the problems of the inner city as they were interested in broader political agendas. By the 1990s, it became apparent for many that infrastructure and homelessness were more pressing local concerns than foreign policy. The ability to see the problems from the global perspective has not come to pass.

What then is the future of municipal foreign policy? Based on the observations of the activists who targeted cities in the 1980s as a way of getting their agendas heard, they have changed their focus. Michael Shuman, a longtime local foreign policy advocate, no longer believes city resolutions are the best method for the advocation of alternative policies: "Frankly, I now discourage resolutions. They are the most symbolic and lukewarm of actions. My sense is that most cities right now can articulate their interests in better ways."[28]

The current administration offers great hope for those interested in the issues examined here. Many feel President Clinton's background as a state governor will make him more responsive to the public. They also see Vice President Al Gore as a strong environmental proponent. Already the president has called for cuts in defense spending and advocated programs of economic conversion to assist displaced military-industrial-complex workers. Shuman cautions, however, that while the kind of confrontational activities that occurred under the Reagan and Bush administrations are no longer on the front burner, should the Clinton administration make a serious foreign policy blunder, it will be faced with city activism. Shuman believes three areas that could reignite the local fires are U.S. military action in Cuba, U.S. ground troop movement into Bosnia without U.N. collective security action, and a resumption of the arms race in the face of a deposition of Yeltsin.[29]

In the meantime, local activists are also pursuing other agendas. They are particularly interested in using the sister city networks as a way to gain inroads and influence policy in other countries. Advocates would argue this strategy was used successfully in the 1980s with Nicaragua. Most recently, *Global Communities,* a publication of the Institute for Policy Studies and successor to the *Bulletin for Municipal Foreign Policy,* advocated the development of sister city ties with Cuba as a means to force both U.S. and Cuban foreign policy.[30] Relationships with El Salvador, South Africa, and Russia have also been promoted in this regard.

Shuman believes this new contact should be a part of community efforts to deal with development and North-South types of issues.[31] These relationships should encourage a development strategy that is less materials intensive and more focused on information and technology transfer. Development of joint environmental programs, demilitarization and economic conversion would all be a part of this activity. There is already a global interest in these relationships with 4,000 cities in 23 countries involved.

Municipal foreign policy is not dead. It remains a vital way for communities to pursue international issues of concern to them and articulate those concerns nationally and internationally. It is unlikely, however, that the movement will be pursued with the same strength it garnered in the 1980s, at least for the next 4 years. There is support for trying direct communication with the new administration as well as dealing with problems at home first. Should neither of these strategies work, there is no doubt that activists will return to the machinery of local governments to get their message heard.

Notes

1. Rimer, S. (1992, July 15). Where only the ocean makes waves. *New York Times,* sec. A, p. 14.

2. Armao, J.-A. (1990, March 27). A movement languishes: Montgomery civic activism loses clout. *Washington Post,* sec. A, p. 1.

3. Davis, M. (1992, October 4). For a city adrift, look to community government. *Los Angeles Times,* sec. M. p. 1.

4. Davis (1992, p. 1).

5. Walls, D. (1993). *The activists almanac.* New York: Simon & Schuster. (Quote from p. 19)

6. Walls (1993, p. 21).

7. Telephone interview with Burt Glass, disarmament campaign director for the SANE/Freeze Education Fund, February 10, 1993.

8. New action resources. (1993, Spring). *PEACE ACTION for a Sane World, 32*(1), 3.

9. Glass (1993).

10. Glass (1993).

11. SANE/Freeze Campaign for Global Security. (1992, June 28). *1992 national congress strategy decisions.* Washington, DC: SANE/Freeze Campaign for Global Security. *Arms Trade Reader* and the video are available from Peace Action for a Sane World (Washington, DC).

12. Glass (1993).

13. Telephone interview with Chuck Johnson, director of Nuclear Free America, February 3, 1993.

14. Nuclear Free America. (1992). *Performance of investments of nuclear weapons contractors vs. the overall stock market: 1986-1991.* Baltimore, MD: Nuclear Free America.

15. The last mile: U.S. communities and South Africa. (1991-1992). *Global Communities,* p. 5.

16. Telephone interview with Richard Knight, February 2, 1993.

17. Knight (1993).

18. Zimmermann, W. (1992, December 14). U.S. refugee assistance programs. *U.S. Department of State Dispatch, 3*(50), 890.

19. Telephone Interview with Darlene Gramena, Chicago Religous Task Force, April 1993.

20. Gramena (1993).

21. For an interesting discussion of some aspects of the legal impact of sanctuary, particularly as they relate to international law, see Hoyt, A. E. (1990). The natural-law claim to sanctuary for Central American refugees. *Loyola of Los Angeles Law Review, 23,*(3) 1023-1053.

22. Gramena (1993).

23. Reinhold, R. (1990, December 12). U.S. judge limits spying at church. *New York Times,* p. A24.

24. Gallup, Jr., G. (1989). *The Gallup poll: Public opinion 1988.* Wilmington, DE: Scholarly Resources, Inc.

25. Gallup, Jr., G. (1993). *The Gallup poll: Public opinion 1992.* Wilmington, DE: Scholarly Resources.

26. Gallup (1993).

27. McDonnell, P. (1990, November 17). Migrant labor: City issue now. *Los Angeles Times,* sec. A, p. 1.

28. Telephone interview with Michael H. Shuman, director of the Institute for Policy Studies, March 15, 1993.

29. Shuman (1993).

30. End the cold war with Cuba. (1992, Autumn). *Global Communities,* pp. 1-8.

31. Shuman (1993).

List of Active Cities by Issue

Comprehensive Test Ban Cities (April 1987)

Alabama
Anniston

Arizona
Tucson

California
Azusa
Costa Mesa
Fremont
Los Angeles
Morgan Hill
Oakland
Redondo Beach
Richmond
Sacramento
San Francisco
San Jose
Santa Cruz
South El Monte
Stockton
Union City
West Covina
West Hollywood

Colorado
Boulder

Denver
Fort Collins

Connecticut
Danbury
Hamden
Hamlin
New Haven
Simsbury
West Hartford

District of Columbia
Washington, D.C.

Georgia
Atlanta

Hawaii
Honolulu
Mauna Loa
Monalulu

Idaho
Hailey
Ketchum

Illinois
Chicago
Urbana

Maine
  Auburn
  Lewiston

Massachusetts
  Ashfield
  Boston
  Brookline
  Cambridge
  Colrain
  Conway
  Cummington
  Deerfield
  Egremont
  Great Barrington
  Greenfield
  Heath
  Lanesboro
  Lenox
  Leverett
  Middlefield
  Monterrey
  Northfield
  Pelham
  Pittsfield
  Richmond
  Sheffield
  Shelbourne
  Shelbourne Falls
  Shutesbury
  Somerville
  South Hadley
  Stockbridge
  Wendell
  West Stockbridge
  Williamsburg
  Williamstown

Michigan
  Detroit
  East Lansing
  Lansing

  Marquette

Minnesota
  Duluth
  Minneapolis

Missouri
  Kansas City
  St. Joseph
  St. Louis

New Hampshire
  Portsmouth

New Jersey
  Audubon
  Belleville
  Camden
  Cape May
  Carney
  Demarest
  East Brunswick
  East Orange
  Englewood
  Ewing Township
  Fair Haven
  Fair Lawn
  Fort Lee
  Hamilton Township
  Highland Park
  Hoboken
  Jersey City
  Kearny
  Lawrenceville
  Leonia
  Long Branch
  Maplewood
  Metuchen
  Montclair
  Newark
  New Brunswick
  North Arlington
  Nutley
  Orange

Paramus
Parsippany-Troy Hills
Princeton Borough
Princeton Township
Ringwood
Roosevelt
Rutherford
South Brunswick
South Orange
Teaneck
Trenton
Wayne
West Orange
Willingboro
Woodbridge

New Mexico
Santa Fe

New York
Chappaqua
Chenango
Johnson City
Mount Vernon
New York City
Scarsdale
Vestal

North Carolina
Edenton

Ohio
Cleveland
Columbus
Yellow Springs
Youngstown

Oregon
Portland

Rhode Island
Bristol
Cranston
Cumberland Hill
Jamestown
Kingston
Narragansett
North Providence
Providence
South Kingston
Warwick
West Kingston
Woonsocket

South Dakota
Brookings

Texas
Austin

Utah
Provo
Riverton
Salt Lake City

Vermont
Burlington

Virginia
Alexandria

Washington
Seattle

Wisconsin
Madison

SOURCE: Nuclear Freeze Weapons Campaign. (1986-1987). 176 jurisdictions now support a comprehensive test ban. *Bulletin of Municipal Foreign Policy, 1*, 17-19.

Nuclear Free Zone Cities (December 1992)

Alaska
Homer*

California
Arcata*
Azusa

Berkeley*
Bolinas*
Carmel-by-the-Sea*
Chico
Claremont
Davis
Del Mar*
Fairfax
Fresno*
Hayward*
Isla Vista
Laguna Beach*
Malibu*
Martinez
Mill Valley
Napa
Oakland*
Placerville
Point Reyes*
St. Helena
San Francisco*
Santa Cruz*
Sausalito
Sebastopol

Colorado
Avon*
Boulder
Jamestown
Telluride

Connecticut
Cornwall*
East Windsor*
Ellington*
Kent*
Salisbury*
Sharon*
Stratford*
Watertown*

Florida
Palm Beach Gardens*

Illinois
Chicago
Evanston
Highland Park*
Lansing
Oak Park*
Park Forest
Wilmette*

Indiana
Miller

Iowa
Bertram*
Iowa City

Kansas
North Newton

Kentucky
Louisville

Maryland
Baltimore*
Garrett Park
Sykesville
Takoma Park
Wilde Lake

Massachusetts
Amherst
Ashfield
Barnstable
Blechertown
Brookline
Chatham
Dennis
Gay Head
Greenfield
Heath
Leverett
Monterrey
Nantucket
New Salem
Newton

Northampton
Princeton*
Provincetown
Sandwich
Shutesbury
Somerville
Stockbridge
Tisbury
Warwick*
Wendell
West Stockbridge
West Tisbury
Williamsburg
Worthington

Michigan
Grandmont
Magnolia

Montana
Missoula*

New Jersey
Camden*
Frankford
Franklin Borough
Hadack
Hardwick Township*
Highland Park
Hoboken
Jersey City
Lafayette Township
Lindenwold*
Roosevelt
Stillwater Township*
Union City
Vernon

New Hampshire
Wolfeboro*

New Mexico
Las Vegas
Taos City

New York
Amenia*
Ellenville
Marcellus*
New York City
Oneonta*
Skyview Acres
Trumansburg*

North Carolina
Chapel Hill*
Durham*
Franklinville

Ohio
Cleveland*
Oberlin
Shaker Heights*
South Euclid*
Warren
Wooster

Oregon
Ashland
Bandon
Eugene*
Florence
Takilma
The Dalles*

Pennsylvania
Birmingham Township*
East Fallowship Township*
Platea Borough*
Union Township
West Chester*

Utah
Springdale*

Vermont
Moretown

Virginia
Charlottesville*
Twin Oaks*

Washington
Bellingham*
Bothell
Leschi
Waldron
Wallingford

Wisconsin
Barksdale
Bayfield
Bayview
Bell
Delta

Keystone
Ladysmith
Lincoln
Madison
Marengo
Marshall Township
Mason
Meadowbrook Township
Morse
Russell
Sun Prairie
Washburn

SOURCES: Nuclear Free Zone Registry. (1986-1987). Now 131 nuclear free zones. *Bulletin of Municipal Foreign Policy*, *1*, 25-26; and Nuclear Free America list of NFZ locations, revised December 2, 1992.
*Cities added since 1987.

Divestment Cities (December 1991)

Arizona
Phoenix
Tucson

California
Berkeley
Davis
East Palo Alto*
Fresno
Hayward*
Los Angeles
Oakland
Palo Alto
Pasadena*
Richmond
Sacramento*
San Diego
San Francisco
San Jose
Santa Barbara
Santa Cruz
Santa Monica*
Stockton

Watsonville*
West Hollywood

Colorado
Boulder
Denver
Fort Collins

Connecticut
Hartford
Middletown
New Haven

Delaware
Wilmington

District of Columbia
Washington

Florida
Gainesville
Miami
Opa Locka*
Orlando*
St. Petersburg*

Tallahassee*
Tampa*

Georgia
Atlanta

Illinois
Chicago

Indiana
Gary*

Iowa
Des Moines

Kansas
Kansas City
Topeka
Witchita*

Louisiana
New Orleans

Maryland
Baltimore
College Park
Takoma Park*

Massachusetts
Amherst
Boston
Brookline
Cambridge
Newton*
Watertown*

Michigan
Ann Arbor
Detroit
East Lansing
Flint
Grand Rapids
Ypsilanti

Minnesota
Minneapolis
St. Paul*

Missouri
Kansas City
St. Louis

Nebraska
Omaha

New Jersey
Atlantic City
Camden
Highland Park*
Jersey City
Newark
Rahway

New York
Freeport
New York
Niagara Falls*
Rochester
Syracuse

North Carolina
Durham
Raleigh

Ohio
Cincinnati
Cleveland
Columbus
Dayton*
Shaker Heights
Toledo*
Youngstown

Pennsylvania
Erie
Harrisburg
Philadelphia
Pittsburgh

South Carolina
Charleston

Texas
Austin*

Dallas*   Newport News*
Ft. Worth*   Portsmouth
Houston   Richmond

Vermont   **Washington**
Burlington   Seattle

Virgina   **West Virginia**
Alexandria   Fairmont
Charlottesville
Hampton*   **Wisconsin**
                                 Madison

SOURCES: The American Committee on Africa. (1987-1988). Jurisdictions passing divestment measures exceed 110. *Bulletin of Municipal Foreign Policy, 2,* 45; City anti-apartheid
action. (1991-1992). *Global Communities,* p. 4.
*Cities added since 1988.

Sanctuary Cities (December 1987)

California   **Minnesota**
Berkeley   Duluth
Davis   Minneapolis
Los Angeles   St. Paul
Oakland
Sacramento   **North Dakota**
San Francisco   Fargo
San Jose   **New Mexico**
Santa Barbara   Santa Fe
Santa Cruz
West Hollywood   **New York**
                                 Ithaca
Colorado   Rochester
Boulder
                                 Pennsylvania
Maryland   Swarthmore
Takoma Park
                                 Vermont
Massachusetts   Burlington
Brookline
Cambridge   **Washington**
                                 Olympia
Michigan   Seattle*
Detroit
East Lansing   **Wisconsin**
                                 Madison

SOURCES: *Basta!* (1986, June); List of sanctuary cities. (1987-1988). *Bulletin of Municipal
Foreign Policy, 2,* 20.
*Rescinded declaration of sanctuary after initial support.

APPENDIX B

Activist City Cases

City	Test	Zone	Divestment	Sanctuary
Arizona				
Tucson	x		x	
California				
Azusa	x	x		
Berkeley		x	x	x
Davis		x	x	x
Fresno		x	x	
Hayward		x	x	
Los Angeles	x		x	x
Oakland	x	x	x	x
Richmond	x		x	
Sacramento	x		x	x
San Francisco	x	x	x	x
San Jose	x		x	x
Santa Barbara			x	x
Santa Cruz	x	x	x	x
Stockton	x		x	
West Hollywood	x		x	x
Colorado				
Boulder	x	x	x	+

City	Test	Zone	Divestment	Sanctuary
Colorado (continued)				
Denver	x		x	
Fort Collins	x		x	
Connecticut				
New Haven	x		x	
District of Columbia				
Washington	x		x	
Georgia				
Atlanta	x		x	
Illinois				
Chicago	x	x	x	
Maryland				
Baltimore		x	x	
Takoma Park		x	x	x
Massachusetts				
Amherst		x	x	
Ashfield	x	x		
Boston	x		x	
Brookline	x	x	x	x
Cambridge	x		x	x
Greenfield	x	x		
Heath	x	x		
Leverett	x	x		
Monterrey	x	x		
Newton		x	x	
Shutesbury	x	x		
Somerville	x	x		
Stockbridge	x	x		
Wendell	x	x		
West Stockbridge	x	x		
Williamsburg	x	x		
Michigan				
Detroit	x		x	x
East Lansing	x		x	x
Minnesota				
Duluth	x			x
Minneapolis	x		x	x
St. Paul			x	x

City	Test	Zone	Divestment	Sanctuary
Missouri				
Kansas City	x		x	
St. Louis	x		x	
New Jersey				
Camden	x	x	x	
Highland Park	x	x	x	
Hoboken	x	x		
Jersey City	x	x	x	
Newark	x		x	
Roosevelt	x	x		
New Mexico				
Sante Fe	x			x
New York				
New York City	x	x	x	+
Rochester			x	x
North Carolina				
Durham		x	x	
Ohio				
Cleveland	x	x	x	
Columbus	x		x	
Shaker Heights		x	x	
Youngstown	x		x	
Texas				
Austin	x		x	
Vermont				
Burlington	x		x	x
Virgina				
Alexandria	x		x	
Washington				
Seattle	x		x	x
Wisconsin				
Madison	x	x	x	x

NOTE: These are cities that have acted on more than one of the four international issues.
+Moved on issue but did not sustain binding action.

APPENDIX C

State and Geographical Distribution of Cities by Activity and Issue

Active Cities (N = 353)

West	Midwest	Northeast	South
1 AK	8 IL	16 CT	1 AL
2 AZ	2 IN	50 MA	1 DE
46 CA	3 IA	2 ME	1 DC
6 CO	4 KS	2 NH	8 FL
3 HI	10 MI	55 NJ	1 GA
2 ID	3 MN	18 NY	1 KY
1 MT	3 MO	10 PA	1 LA
3 NM	1 NE	12 RI	6 MD
7 OR	1 ND	2 VT	5 NC
4 UT	13 OH		1 SC
7 WA	1 SD		4 TX
	17 WI		7 VA
			1 WV
Totals			
82 (23%)	66 (19%)	167 (47%)	38 (11%)

Activist Cities ($N = 67$)

West	Midwest	Northeast	South
1 AZ	1 IL	1 CT	1 DC
16 CA	2 MI	15 MA	1 GA
3 CO	3 MN	6 NJ	2 MD
1 NM	2 MO	2 NY	1 NC
1 WA	4 OH	1 VT	1 TX
	1 WI		1 VA
Totals			
22 (33%)	13 (19.4%)	25 (37.3%)	7 (10.4%)

Comprehensive Test Ban Cities ($N = 160$)

West	Midwest	Northeast	South
1 AZ	2 IL	6 CT	1 AL
17 CA	4 MI	32 MA	1 DC
3 CO	2 MN	2 ME	1 GA
3 HI	3 MO	1 NH	1 NC
2 ID	5 OH	44 NJ	1 TX
1 NM	1 SD	7 NY	1 VA
1 OR	1 WI	12 RI	
3 UT		1 VT	
Totals			
31 (19%)	18 (11%)	105 (66%)	6 (4%)

Nuclear Free Zone Cities ($N = 159$)

West	Midwest	Northeast	South
1 AK	7 IL	8 CT	1 FL
26 CA	1 IN	29 MA	1 KY
4 CO	2 IA	1 NH	5 MD
1 MT	1 KS	14 NJ	3 NC
2 NM	2 MI	7 NY	2 VA
6 OR	6 OH	5 PA	
1 UT	17 WI	1 VT	
5 WA			
Totals			
46 (29%)	36 (23%)	65 (41%)	12 (7%)

Divestment Cities (N = 103)

West	Midwest	Northeast	South
2 AZ	1 IL	3 CT	1 DE
20 CA	1 IN	6 MA	1 DC
3 CO	1 IA	6 NJ	7 FL
1 WA	3 KS	5 NY	1 GA
	6 MI	4 PA	1 LA
	2 MN	1 VT	3 MD
	2 MO		2 NC
	1 NE		1 SC
	6 OH		4 TX
	1 WI		6 VA
			1 WV
Totals			
26 (25%)	24 (23%)	25 (24%)	28 (27%)

Sanctuary Cities (N = 28)

West	Midwest	Northeast	South
10 CA	2 MI	2 MA	1 MD
1 CO	3 MN	2 NY	
2 WA	1 ND	1 PA	
1 NM	1 WI	1 VT	
Totals			
14 (50%)	7 (25%)	6 (21%)	1 (4%)

Suggested Reading

Alger, C. F. (1977). "Foreign" policies of U.S. publics. *International Studies Quarterly, 21,* 277-319.

Alger, C. F. (1985, June). *Creating local institutions for sustained participation in peace building.* Paper presented at 8th annual meeting of the International Society of Political Psychology, Washington, D.C.

Alger, C. F., & Mendlovitz, S. (1985, March). *Approaches to global issues by local activists in the United States.* Paper presented at the 26th annual convention of the International Studies Association, Washington, D.C.

Almond, G. A. (1988). The return to the state. *American Political Science Review, 82,* 853-874.

Bancroft, R. L. (1974). *America's mayors and councilmen: Their problems and frustrations.* Washington: National League of Cities.

Banfield, E. C. (1970). *The unheavenly city: The nature and future of our urban crisis.* Boston: Little, Brown.

Banfield, E. C., & Wilson, J. Q. (1963). *City politics.* New York: Vintage.

Bau, I. (1985). *This ground is holy: Church sanctuary and Central American refugees.* New York: Paulist.

Browning, R. P., Marshall, D. R., & Rabb, D. H. (1984). *Protest is not enough: The struggle of blacks and Hispanics for equality in urban politics.* Berkeley: University of California Press.

Caporaso, J. A. (1982, December). *Theoretical framework for the study of Canadian-American relations in the 1980s* (rev.). Paper prepared for the Research Group on Canadian-American Relations, Harvard University, Cambridge, MA.

Clavel, P. (1986). *The progressive city: Planning and participation, 1969-1984.* New Brunswick, NJ: Rutgers University Press.

Clavel, P., & Wiewel, W. (Eds.). (1991). *Harold Washington and the neighborhoods: Progressive city government in Chicago, 1983-1987.* New Brunswick, NJ: Rutgers University Press.

Crain, R. L., Katz, E., & Rosenthal, D. B. (1969). *The politics of community conflict: The fluoridation decision.* Indianapolis: Bobbs-Merrill.

Cunningham, J. V. (1970). *Urban leadership in the sixties: Approaches to the study of violence.* Waltham, MA: Brandeis University, Lemberg Center for the Study of Violence.

Dahl, R. A. (1961). *Who governs? Democracy and power in an American City.* New Haven, CT: Yale University Press.

Danielson, M. N. (1971). *Metropolitan politics: A reader* (2nd ed.). Boston: Little, Brown.

Dilldine, D. A., Eason, B., Frendries, J. P., Larson, D. J., Lesure, M. J., Parsons, J., Powers, R., Powers, R. M., Puissant, R. E., Vertz, L., Weintrob, N., & Zmrozek, J. (1978). *A bibliography of case studies of bosses and machines.* Monticello, IL: Vance Bibliography.

Dye, T. R. (1966). *Politics, economics, and the public: Policy outcomes in the American states.* Chicago: Rand McNally.

Dye, T. R. (1985). *Politics in states and communities* (5th ed.). Englewood Cliffs, NJ: Prentice-Hall.

Dye, T. R., & Hawkins, B. W. (Eds.). (1971). *Politics in the metropolis: A reader in conflict and cooperation.* Columbus, OH: Merrill.

Farkus, S. (1971). *Urban lobbying: Mayors in the federal arena.* New York: New York Union Press.

Feagin, J. R. (1985, March). *The transformation of Houston in world perspective: Toward a theory of city specialization.* Paper presented at the 26th annual convention of the International Studies Association, Washington, DC.

Freeman, L. C. (1965). *Elementary applied statistics.* New York: Wiley.

Hadden, J. K., & Borgatta, E. F. (1965). *American cities: Their social characteristics.* Chicago: Rand McNally.

Hahn, H. (1970). Correlates of public sentiments about war: Local referenda on the Vietnam issue. *American Political Science Review, 64,* 1186-1198.

Haider, D. H. (1974). *When governments come to Washington.* New York: The Free Press.

Harrigan, J. J. (1981). *Political change in the metropolis* (2nd ed.). Boston: Little, Brown.

Hawkins, B. W. (1971). *Politics and urban policies.* Indianapolis: Bobbs-Merrill.

Helmer, J., & Eddington, N. A. (Eds.). (1973). *Urbanman: The psychology of urban survival.* New York: The Free Press.

Henkin, L. (1972). *Foreign affairs and the Constitution.* Mineola, NY: Foundation Press.

Holli, M. G., & Jones, P. d'A. (1981). *Biographical dictionary of American mayors, 1820-1980.* Westport, CT: Greenwood Press.

Holsti, O. R., & Rosenau, J. N. (1984). *American leadership in world affairs: Vietnam and the breakdown of consensus.* Boston: Allen & Unwin.

Howitt, A. M. (1977, September). *Mayors and policy innovation* (Urban Planning Policy Analysis and Administration, Discussion Paper D77-13).

Cambridge, MA: Harvard University, Department of City and Regional Planning, Harvard University.

Keohane, R. O., & Nye, J. S., Jr. (1987). Power and interdependence revisited. *International Organization, 41,* 725-753.

Keohane, R. O., & Nye, J. S., Jr. (Eds.). (1972). *Transnational relations and world politics.* Cambridge, MA: Harvard University Press.

Kline, J. M. (1984). The expanding international agenda for state governments. *State Government, 57,* 2-6.

Long, N. (1972). *The unwalled city: Reconstituting the urban community.* New York: Basic Books.

Lotchin, R. W. (Ed.). *The martial metropolis: U.S. cities in war and peace.* New York: Praeger.

Love, J. (1984, March). *State and local governments in international affairs.* Paper presented at the 25th annual convention of the International Studies Association, Atlanta.

Moreno, D. (1990). *U.S. policy in Central America: The endless debate.* Miami: Florida International University Press.

Mueller, J. E. (1977). Changes in American public attitudes toward international involvement. In E. P. Stern (Ed.), *The limits of military intervention* (pp. 323-344). Beverly Hills, CA: Sage.

Nordlinger, E. A., Lowi, T. J., & Fabbrini, S. (1988). The return to the state: Critiques. *American Political Science Review, 82,* 875-904.

Padover, S. K. (1968). *The living U.S. Constitution* (rev. ed.). New York: New American Library.

Pasley, J. L. (1987, June 22). Twisted sisters: Foreign policy for fun and profit. *The New Republic, 196,* 14-18.

Peterson, P. E. (Ed.). (1985). *The new urban reality.* Washington, DC: The Brookings Institution.

Pressman, J. (1972). Preconditions of mayoral leadership. *American Political Science Review, 66,* 511-524.

Raymond, J. (1985, January 17). South African divestment: Breaking up is hard to do. *Santa Barbara News & Review,* pp. 5-7.

Rodwin, L., & Hollister, R. M. (Eds.). (1984). *Cities of the mind: Images and themes of the city in the social sciences.* New York: Plenum Press.

Rosenau, J. N. (1980). *The study of global interdependence: Essays on the transnationalisation of world affairs.* New York: Nichols.

Ruchelman, L. I. (Ed.). (1969). *Big city mayors: The crisis in urban politics.* Bloomington: Indiana University Press.

Scott, M. (1985). *The San Francisco Bay Area: A metropolis in perspective* (2nd ed.). Berkeley: University of California Press.

Sharkansky, I. (1968). *Spending in the American states.* Chicago: Rand McNally.

Tabb, W. K., & Sawers, L. (1984). *Marxism and the metropolis* (2nd ed.). New York: Oxford University Press.

Winter, W. O. (1981). *State and local government in a decentralized republic.* New York: Macmillan.

Zisk, B. H. (1973). *Local interest politics: A one-way street.* Indianapolis: Bobbs-Merrill.

Index

About the Author

Heidi H. Hobbs is currently an Assistant Professor of Political Science at Illinois State University. She received her Ph.D. in International Relations from the University of Southern California. Her areas of research and teaching interests are international relations and foreign policy analysis. Her recent publications include articles on the breakup of Yugoslavia in *Studies in Conflict and Terrorism* and the role of nonstate sectors in foreign policy in *State 2000: A New Model for Managing Foreign Affairs.* She is an active member of the International Studies Association and currently serves as the President of the Foreign Policy Analysis section of that organization.